DEEP COVER

BESTSELLING AUTHOR

PETE THRON

Acknowledgments

I thank my Ocean Ave, Brooklyn friends, Nick Siano, and Lita Prevete. My beta reader and inspiration for the character Kelly is Kelly Hightower. My amazing beta reader Sharon Baum spent countless hours helping me with this book. Bo Silverman for his knowledge of Harley-Davidson motorcycles, the biker world, his photography, and his artwork. My talented nonstop working agent, Heidi R. Hedquist. Thank you all for helping me with this project and furthering my career.

Dedication

This book is dedicated to Andrea Miles Rhoads. Heaven has gained a literary angel. Thank you for always being an incredible friend and mentor. You're greatly missed.

I

Ripper

Summer of 2022, Marine Park, New York. Hatchet, the Brooklyn Chapter President of the Excaliburs called church in the clubhouse. (I'll explain what church means later.)

"Alright brothers, the mother chapter is riding into Brooklyn today to collect their dues for the quarter, so have your fucking shit together. "He yelled in my direction.

"Prospect, clean up the clubhouse and make sure the bar is stocked to the hilt. Also, put an order into Phil's Hero and have them cater the party. Prospect you'll be under the spotlight today so don't fuck anything up. And for your own sake, try to stay clear of that crazy fucker Ripper. He's doing everything he can to try and make you quit or dig up dirt on you. He has no idea what you've been through and what you've done for our country when you were in the military. But we do and we've got your back, Rick. Just do what you have to and you'll be patched in soon. Remember I'm your sponsor so don't make me look bad."

"You got it, Pres."

Ripper was the Sergeant at Arms of the Mother Chapter and was one of the most vicious bastards in the club. Hatchet was so right, that fucker, broke my balls every chance he had. I wanted to nail him to the cross.

I cleaned up the clubhouse and got things ready for the party. The roar of six Harley-Davidsons came riding into the compound. I was fetching beers for the patched members when I heard Ripper yelling for me.

"Prospect go get me a beer and one of those hero sandwiches. Fucking make sure it doesn't have mustard on it. And make sure the beer is ice cold. Now hurry the fuck up."

"On it Ripper.

"Hold on there, jerk-off"

Ripper waved for me to come closer to him. I stood an arm's distance away from his foul-smelling breath and his brown, yellow, stained teeth. It smelled like total dog shit. I'm sure his mouth hadn't seen a toothbrush in the last ten years. His arms were muscular and sleeved out with prison tattoos, just like most of those shithead drug-dealing bastards. He looked just like the wrestler Kevin Nash but bigger and much more menacing.

"I don't like you, Ricky boy. Did your chapter President tell you that you're never going to get patched in, prospect?

"No Ripper, he didn't."

With that, he sent a punch into my solar plexus knocking the wind out of me. On any other given day, I would have quickly blocked his punch and possibly broken his forearm but I couldn't hit a patched member without the President of my chapter or the Mother Club's permission to defend myself. I drew a deep breath in and went on my way to bring that cocksucker his food and beer.

Several hours later Ripper yelled to the members that were sniffing crank and drinking beers. "Let's go into the backyard and throw some axes and knives."

The short handle axe was the club's weapon of choice. Most members carried a handheld hatchet or a splitting axe. They carried them in their saddlebags on their bikes so they didn't get a weapon charge. Many of the members carried throwing axes and were pretty fucking good at hitting a target at close range. Thanks to my Ranger training. I'd become an expert in knife fighting and throwing edged weapons. I could hit a target at twenty to thirty yards.

We headed outside waiting for the Mother Chapter's President, to give the okay to start throwing axes. But before Arthur said anything, Ripper grabbed my leather vest from behind and whipped me around to face him. I was surrounded by twenty Excaliburs. All I could think of was. *Is this it? Am I going to get whacked by a bunch of overweight, muscle-bound, greasy tattooed, bearded criminals?"*

Ripper got right into my face; we were nose to nose. He was an inch from mine.

"Alright Rick, where did you do your fucking cop training? I know you're the fucking fuzz. You're an undercover cop, aren't you? You fucking pig cock sucker. I know you have a wire on you and I'm going to find it.

And when I do, I'm going to waste your ass right where you're fucking standing. I'm asking you a fucking question. Where did you get trained, prospect?"

"What the hell are you talking about, Ripper? I'm not a cop or anything else. I hate the fucking pigs and feds. Just as much as you."

Ripper said. "Give me your cut prospect."

"That's not happening, Ripper. You want it, you'll have to take it off of me. I die with this on." I stood up straight, unclenching my fist. "So, fuck you,"

Ripper drew his knife from his hip and put it against my throat. But before he tried to cut me, I'd have that blade sticking into his left eye socket in less than a second.

"Enough, Ripper." Arthur walked out and said. "Prospect, I'm giving you permission to remove your cut without any penalty against you. Remove it now."

I looked over at my Pres and he nodded. I handed my cut to Arthur.

Ripper smiled. "Now strip mother fucker."

I took off my white t-shirt to reveal that I wasn't wearing a wire. The members surrounding me couldn't stop staring at the Special Forces tattoo skull wearing the beret and the lightning bolt coming out the sides and an arrow through the skull head. Their eyes moved to the Navy Seal Trident. The eagle holding the trident and flintlock pistol. They took a long look at the long scar that ran across my back from an Isis soldier's blade. Scars from the shrapnel of a bomb that I had used my body as a shield to protect a few of my brothers. That scar was on my back. I turned around as they looked at my chest and lower abdomen where more scars and several bullet holes covered my chest. Just to go the extra mile I dropped my pants and underwear to prove that I wasn't wearing a wire.

Hatchet laughed, "Holy fucking shit prospect get dressed."

He walked over to Arthur and handed him a brew. "I told you this guy was a fucking war hero. Please, with all due respect, keep your dog on a leash. He's the best prospect my chapter has ever had."

I got dressed and Ripper told me to hang some targets on the trees. While I was hanging up the last target on a tree, the whoop, whoop, of a flying axe whizzed past my head. I didn't even flinch when the axe landed on the tree. The members freaked out from my lack of reaction.

Hatchet yelled at Ripper, "What the fuck are you doing? He's a brother, you crazy mother fuck."

Ripper said. "That cop ain't no brother of mine and never will be. He's the fucking police or a rat and if he takes any of us down I'm going to kill you first Hatchet."

I turned to Arthur and asked for permission to speak. He nodded yes, and I went over to Ripper and said. "If and when I get patched in. You and me are going to go a few rounds in the pit mother fucker. That I can guarantee you."

"Bring it on cocksucker."

I motioned to Hatchet to hand me his throwing axe and he tossed it over. Then I turned and threw the axe toward the target, hitting it dead center.

I said to Ripper and the other members, "If you're going to kill a target, make sure you fucking do it right."

II

The Call

A certain One Percenter club in New York had become the target of the New York Bureau of Narcotics (NYBN) and I would become the first undercover agent in the bureau to try and infiltrate the deadly OMG on the East Coast. That OMG was the Excaliburs who had several chapters along the East Coast. I would later learn that they had made several attempts to expand the club into the West Coast but were warned by the predominant MCs not to set foot in San Francisco, LA, or anywhere else for that matter on the West Coast. My name is Special Agent Rick Volpe, AKA Rick Mason. Before I became an agent with NYBN, I served in the military for ten years. Six in the Army with Special Forces.

My branch was the Army Ranger Special Forces Regiment. After my six years had been completed with the Army I signed up with the Navy and became a Navy Seal. I'd become the first person in history to ever join two of the most respected branches in U.S. history. Between these two elite groups, I'd completed ninety-nine missions successfully. While in Special Forces one mission, I hadn't been so lucky and was captured behind enemy lines in the Middle East. Only to be rescued by Seal Team Six. Which prompted me to become a Navy Seal. I had been tortured for several days when the teams came bursting through the enemy compound to bring me safely home to my beautiful wife Kelly.

May 10, 2021, I was filling out the last field report of an eighteen-month-long investigation where I'd been working undercover as Rick Mason infiltrating a White American Resistance movement that had a charter in Upstate New York near Bear Mountain. They're a White Supremacy group that believes that white people are superior to those of other races and should dominate them all.

I'd been able to become a member of that group and in time had risen in the ranks to become the secretary-treasurer of the charter. I played the role to a tee. I even went as far as to shave my head bald, which my wife Kelly loved. Being the secretary-treasurer had given me all the leeway I needed to get photos of their strict ledger which documented all the illegal weapons and drugs they had purchased on the dark web. I also purchased a cache of weapons from another anti-American group during the investigation. In the cache was a rocket launcher, twenty hand grenades, and fifty M16 fully automatic rifles.

The group I was working with had sold weapons of mass destruction to other anti-American organizations looking to disrupt the government and wreak havoc on its law-abiding citizens. The ledger also kept detailed records of each member and the dues that were paid by each member to the leader. In the last month of the investigation, the president of the organization had called a meeting of the council. He advised us that they were planning on bombing the FBI office in Manhattan.

After the meeting, I immediately notified my field office from a secure location and told them to raid the compound at 3:00 AM the next day when everyone would be sleeping. I had my supervisor inform the FBI of any possible bombs and alert ATF to perform sweeps of the entire building to locate any suspicious packages or explosive devices that had already been put into place at the building or the underground garage.

The raids were conducted and completed without any law enforcement casualties. The operation was an enormous success and we had been able to confiscate several caches of weapons, twenty-two bombs, and one hundred kilos of cocaine. A total of thirty-two members were arrested including the president and the vice president of the charter.

After I completed all the necessary paperwork I raced home to my wife Kelly and three children. We had two girls, Mary and Carol, and our son Vincent. The girls are twins they're twelve years of age. Vincent is ten years old. I'd been away for two long months and wanted to wrap my arms around the kids and finally have my stunning wife back in my arms. We lived in a four-bedroom house in Bronxville, New York. The house had been left to me by my late Aunt Dot.

I pulled my 1972 Midnight Blue AMX which was named Defiant around the corner of our home and walked quietly to our front door and rang the bell. I could hear the kids playing and watching the Saturday morning cartoons. Kelly looked through the peephole and quickly unlocked the locks and chain and threw the door open. She jumped into my arms and wrapped herself around me and we had a long passionate kiss.

"Rick, you could've told me you were coming home. I would've made you a big breakfast." She said,

"Babe, I missed you and the kids so much, I just raced home to be with you all."

The kids jumped into my arms and we had one of the greatest weekends I could remember. During the night Kelly and I couldn't wait to be in each other's arms. Monday morning came too quickly for my liking. I cleaned up and trimmed my goatee.

I yelled down to Kelly. "Should I let my hair grow back in or shave my head?"

Kelly said. "Don't you dare. I love it that way."

My cell phone rang and I asked Kelly, "Babe, can you see who that is please."

She answered and said, "Hello, Agent Volpe's, answering service how may I help you? Oh, hi Jim, how are things with you and the family? Okay, I'll go and get him."

"It's your boss Hun."

"Morning Jimbo, what's up?"

"Hey, brother, how would you like a shot at taking down the OMG the Excaliburs MC? I have an informant that called into the office a few days ago. She's from one of their support clubs. You know, The Centurions. She's agreed to make an introduction to the Excaliburs. This one is a bit of a tweaker. She had a run-in with one of the Excalibur members who busted her up a little. So, she wants payback. You know the kind of knucklehead that wants a quick payday and gets the hell out of dodge."

"Jimbo, I just finished that long investigation with the White American Resistance movement. Give me a day to speak with my wife about this. I'll be in on Tuesday; I'm resting for the rest of the day. You know some quality family time."

"Listen, Rick, you're the only agent I would even think of putting inside that scumbag OMG." (*Outlaw Motorcycle Gang*).

"I'll meet you at the Merrick Diner at 1:00 PM Tuesday, Jimbo. I know it's a bit of a haul for you from downtown Manhattan. But if you want me to even consider doing this then it's going to cost you a nice lunch."

I hung up the phone and my mood quickly shifted into a low-spirited one. Kelly could see the look of dread in my eyes and came over to me and hugged me tightly.

She said, "You're going back under, aren't you?"

"I haven't decided yet. We need to talk about this and think it through. Weigh out all of our options, the good and bad. This would be a very **Deep Cover** operation if we decide to do this. This organization is brutal and extremely violent."

Kelly asked, "Who are you going after?" I said, "The Excalibur MC."

My wife had recently retired from the Suffolk County Police Department a year ago as a Second Grade Detective. She'd done her twenty years of service and got out to let me perform my duty as a federal agent. We had met while I was on vacation from one of my ops with the Rangers. Kelly had been involved in many undercover operations during her time as a cop and knew all the risks and rewards when it came to going undercover.

Kelly said, " Rick, I love you and know you can take these bastards down. You need to do this. They need to be stopped with all the drug dealing and killing they're committing in Brooklyn. I say go for it. I've got it handled with the kids. We'll be fine. You make sure you come home to us in one piece and yourself, not some scumbag outlaw biker."

The kids finished eating their breakfast and headed to school. I looked at my stunning wife and whispered in her ear. "I want you so badly, right now."

We couldn't get upstairs quickly enough. We ripped each other's clothes off and made passionate love. We lay entangled with each other and the two dogs jumped onto the bed with us. They wanted to go for a walk. Both of the dogs were huge Belgian German Shepherds. Kelly had opted to go into K9 her last two years on the job and she loved being a dog handler…K9 cop.

Her dog's name is Talia. She was a bomb and narcotic dog and she also recovered cadavers. The other dog was mine. On my last tour, I decided to go into the K9 division of the Seals. My first Seal dog's name was Rocco and he was a bomb locator. He was with me during a bombing in the Middle East and I took some shrapnel in my back. The dog took shrapnel in his side, it punctured his lung, and he died on the battlefield next to me. He'd taken most of the blast and saved my unit leader and best friend Leo Steele AKA (Kahuna) life. My Seal team grabbed Rocco and I and took us out of the kill zone, then drove us to the hospital.

Rocco was given the Medal of Honor the next day. I had the dog flown back home and Uncle Bobby and Kelly buried him in our backyard. Years later a member of Seal Team Six knocked on our door with a baby Belgian Shephard pup that was supposed to be trained to be a K9 for the Seals. The members of the teams asked their CO if they could send the dog to me as a token of my service.

I gave them a huge thank you and Kelly and I trained Ronin to be a badass K9 dog that performs all types of duties that a K9 dog would perform for any police department or the Military. Both dogs protected our family with their lives. They are gentle giants around my kids, Kelly, and me. But God forbid a person broke into the house. They would tear them to shreds.

I said to Kelly. "I need to visit Uncle Bobby at the shop. I'm going to need his insight on this. I'll be back at 6:00 tonight and we'll take the kids to Vincent's restaurant for some Italian food. Babe, always remember, "My love for you will never end."

Kelly pointed at her right eye, then her heart, and then pointed back at me. It was our way of saying; "I love you to each other." I took the dogs for a quick walk and then showered and headed over to Uncle Bobby's bike shop, Hog's City in Levittown NY. He's owned the shop for the past thirty years. I'd practically grown up inside there. Uncle Bobby had become a second father to me and taught me everything I needed to know about tearing down a Harley Davidson bike and rebuilding it.

He'd raised me when my parents had died in a car accident. The man didn't hesitate. The day of the funeral he took my hand and welcomed me into his home as his son. He taught me how to identify every part of a Harley-Davidson, every make, and model. He was a master mechanic and an incredible salesman. He was also an expert in driving a Harley. Many of the One Percenters went to his shop for his advice and expertise on fixing their bikes.

As I walked through the front door of the shop, my uncle was elated to see me. He said, "Look what the cat dragged in." "How goes it, Ricky boy? How are the G-Men treating you?"

"All is good Uncle Bobby. We need to talk and I'm going to need a bike to ride during an investigation into a certain one percenter club. I'm hoping it won't be too long of an investigation. Just a loner if you're okay with that."

Little did I know I'd be riding with the Excaliburs for the next eighteen months.

Uncle Bobby said. "Well, I just so happened to be working on your birthday present and it's ready now. Let's talk about this before you jump into this crazy assignment. So, I can explain to you what the hell you're getting yourself into. Maybe I can be of some assistance to you and your investigation."

He opened the back door to the shop and he said. "Here she is bud. It's a 1982 Harley Davidson Electric Glide. I had them paint it red with a little white. Every part is brand new. You have a Slate Saddlemen SDC custom seat for long rides and the tires are Metzler 888 Ultra Marathons. I also installed a kill switch. That way no one can steal your ride. It's located under the front seat. When you're getting on and off your bike just make it look like you're using the front of the seat to help you on and off of her. It's one badass bike son. She's all yours bud."

"Holy mother of God this is a beast of a ride Uncle Bobby. I have no words. Can we go for a ride?"

"Fuck yea let's ride, Ricky boy. First, here's another little present from me." He handed me a Schott Perfecto Leather Jacket and a black matte helmet.

"Jeez Uncle Bobby, you didn't have to do all of this for me."

"Yes, I did, your boss, Jimbo, called me a few days ago and explained to me that he was going to ask you to go undercover with the Excaliburs. You know that they're sworn enemies are good friends of mine. The Guardians Chapter in New York. You've got to be real fucking careful if you travel down this road kiddo. You're going to need all of your martial art skills and your military training. Those fuckers are ruthless killers."

Uncle Bobby kickstarted his 1946 Harley-Davidson Knucklehead and it turned over on the third kick. I fired up my Harley and we rode out to Jones Beach. The bike was a complete monster and handled the turns perfectly and hugged the straightaways with beautiful traction. I was elated and knew I needed to return the gesture by getting him an incredible gift.

Uncle Bobby said. "Let's take a break at the Circle M diner." We downed a few deluxe cheeseburgers and after we finished the last of our fries, Uncle Bobby said.

" Rick, you just make sure you come home in one piece and yourself. I don't want you falling for any of that One Percenter stuff. I know the life and it can drag you into some very dark places. If you have to rely on your training then so be it. If you get engaged in a physical altercation use your martial arts training. You've got to protect yourself by any means necessary.

Remember never strike a patched member. If you get to the prospecting stage. You'll have to take all the punishment they dole out. Strike back only if you've been given the go by your president or your sponsor. Bar fights are another thing. Kick ass if you have to. Let's get the hell home. I have another bike to finish rebuilding."

"Thanks, Uncle Bobby, I appreciate everything you've ever done for me."

"It was my pleasure bud. You're my son, always remember that. Give the kids and that pretty wife, Kelly a big kiss and hug for me."

III

The Hang Around

The next morning, I woke up around 5:00 AM from the clock in my head and went downstairs to train on the wooden man. That piece of equipment is essential in my Kung Fu training. I'd reached my black belt status in Kung Fu and my Dan level, which is the equivalent of a black belt level in Aki Jujitsu. I was a 4th Dan in that art. I tried to train five days a week in both arts along with my physical conditioning. I relied on my old Navy Seal workout to keep me fit and ready for action. It wasn't easy for me to keep up with my training when I was working a case and performing as the undercover.

I sent my forearms into the thick wooden pegs and then several punches dead center into the tree-like pole. Then four shin kicks into the mid-section of the wooden man then a round house dead center into it. I released the locking mechanism and enabled the contraption to spin as I struck it. This was done to help me train blocks with both my forearms and lower legs. The training session lasted twenty minutes. I turned to head back upstairs but was surprised to see Kelly had been watching me hit the hell out of the wooden man.

She said, "You know how much I love watching you train? Mind if I have a go at him?"

I said. "Please do my love."

Kelly was also a black belt in Jeet Kune Do. The martial art that the famous Bruce Lee invented. The woman was a complete badass fighter. I was always glad that she was on my side and protecting the kids while I was on assignments. When she was through with her training she sat on the basement steps beside me and said.

"Rick, you've got to be really careful with these guys. They're the real deal. I did some research on them and had my old team send me some past incident reports. These bastards are either involved in or accused of serious violent felonies. The file is upstairs. Let's go up and get some coffee and I'll whip you up some waffles and bacon. Then we can take a look at the reports. You can use that photographic memory of yours to store the information that you see in the files."

For those who aren't familiar with what a photographic memory is. It's the memory and total recall, and I have the gift to recall an image from memory with high precision after seeing it only once and without using a mnemonic device. I can study manuals, textbooks, and pretty much anything I look at and commit to memory. It comes in quite handy during investigations where I don't feel safe wearing a wire or recording device. It had also come in handy during all the secret operations I was involved in with the Rangers and Seals. I took a shower and was getting dressed when my son Vincent came into the room and asked.

"Pops, will you be home for my game this weekend? I'm pitching. Maybe after you can make me some cooks. That's his way of saying homemade chocolate chip cookies."

"Sure, thing son. I wouldn't miss it for anything and I'll make some cooks tonight for you and your sisters. And I'll pick up some ice cream and Reese's Peanut Butter Cups for Mom."

My son was staring at all the battle scars on my back, chest, and abdomen. There's a piece of shrapnel still inside me which is pressing on my lower lumbar. The doctors refused to remove it due to the concern it would cripple me if they attempted to do so. It accounted for a lot of my back pain. The spoils of war. I headed to the diner at 12:30 where Jimbo had already downed his second cup of coffee.

Jimbo said, "I took the liberty of ordering you the cheeseburger deluxe. Rick. how the hell have you been? I did a once-over on the reports you filed the other day. Fucking outstanding work. You're going to get your own team after this investigation is over Rick. I'm going to make damn sure of that. Is that the bike Bobby built for you out in the parking lot? That guy is a wizard when it comes to bikes. You, going to let me ride it afterward?"

"Damn boss, you just shot a thousand questions at me. Slow down. And sorry, that's a big no and another no, on you riding my bike. Uncle Bobby would string me up by my balls if someone else rode her and then crashed it. I can give you a ride and really open her up if you'd like."

Jimbo laugh and said, "Damn Rick, you have a dirty mind. Let's get to it while we're drinking our coffee. I have two jackets I want you to study. One is on those lowlife bastards the Excaliburs and the other is on the Centurions.

"You've got to watch your six with these two clubs brother. They're extremely dangerous and will kill you in a heartbeat if they make you."

I informed Jim. "I know about several of them. Kelly's old team sent her a dossier on the two MCs. The Caliburs are one fucked up biker gang. They're involved in some heavy shit from what I've read. I'll need you on the backup team at all times Jimbo and we have to hand-pick the two teams that will be on this case with us. I need good solid drivers that know how to ghost me while I'm riding with those crazy fucks."

Jimbo said, "I've got your six and have the perfect team. You'll be safe brother. All of them know how to tail a UC (undercover). You've done a few cases with them already. The MCs won't even know we're behind you or in the vicinity of where you're at. Alrighty, the CI (confidential informant) will meet us tomorrow night at Club 40 in Merrick. It's right next to the Church on Merrick Avenue. I told her to be there around 9:00 pm."

I said. "Alright, Jimbo let's give it a shot and see where this leads us. What's this chick look like, brother?"

He said, "That's my surprise for you. It'll be fine Rick. I wouldn't lead you astray. You've got this bud. Talk to you tomorrow. Have a good day off and give everyone a hug for me. We have to get together for dinner soon."

With that, he grabbed the check and paid the waitress. I finished my food, hopped onto my bike, and decided to ride for a little while to get a better feel for her. I took the Meadowbrook Parkway and gunned it for a straight twenty miles. I hit speeds of 100 miles per hour and it felt incredible. I felt so free and alive. My only regret was that Kelly wasn't on the back of the bike experiencing what I was.

I arrived home at 5:00 pm and the kids, dogs, and Kelly came out to greet me as I was getting off my bike. Carol, Mary, and Vincent wanted a ride on the bike. I looked at Kelly and she nodded that it was ok.

She said, "I'll call Vincent's and tell them we'll be there by seven Hun."

I blew her a kiss and said. "Thanks, sweetheart. Now let me give these rugrats a ride."

First Carol went. Then Mary and last was Vincent. He got the biggest kick out of it. The boy had a lot of his mother and father in him. He liked the thrill of adventure and danger. The kids were all black belts in Jeet Kune Do.

Kelly took them to her Sensi's dojo twice a week like clockwork. She also was going for her fourth-degree black belt in the Fall. I was looking forward to seeing that and the kids advancing. She told the kids that it would be their choice if they wanted to continue their training when they reached the age of 16. I know what many parents think.

"Instead of teaching your kids how to fight and mangle other kids, they should be in Girl Scouts and Boy Scouts. Well, they happen to be in those also and they play sports."

I had to hand it to Kelly, she's a true mom warrior. She still trains the dogs with all of their K9 exercises and makes them find and locate things to keep them sharp. She has a dog trainer from the Suffolk P.D. come to the house once a month to wear the bite sleeve, bite suit, and bite collar. He drops off scent aids to reinforce their scent training. The kids hide in crazy places and put the scent aids on them for the dog to locate them. It's a game for all of them but it also keeps Ronin and Talia sharp as hell.

The dogs never leave the kids or Kelly's side when their outside of the house with them. We could walk them without a leash but we choose to use them just to be safe. Two years ago, I'd purchased a candy apple red 1968 Ford Mustang GT for Kelly for her 42nd birthday. It was her retirement gift. We took both cars to Vincents so the kids could be in the cars while we raced down the Parkway. We had a blast. Both the Javelin and Mustang were beasts of cars and we maintained them to a high performance level. Mary and Vincent rode with Kelly and Carol rode with me.

The dinner was incredible. We shared the fried calamari, mozzarella sticks, baked clams, and an antipasto salad for appetizers. Kelly and I had stuffed shells and the kids ordered baked ziti. Then came the dessert. Homemade cannoli's, tiramisu, and napoleons. Kelly ordered tea and I ordered the Lavazza premium coffee. We even ordered another basket of bread to dip into the olive oil. What a meal. We stayed in the restaurant for close to three hours. I knew the owner Vincenzo and I took the time out to thank him for the amazing meal and hospitality.

That night was amazing in the bedroom, to say the least. We went at it for hours. We only stopped to re-energize with a few Red Bulls and water. Kelly just got more beautiful with each passing moment and we were true soulmates from the beginning. I knew I was the luckiest man alive and I loved it.

The next morning, I downed six over-medium eggs, several pieces of turkey bacon, two slices of rye toast, and three cups of coffee. The kids finished their cereal, kissed Kelly, and me goodbye, and were off to school. I fed Ronin and Talia then Kelly and I walked them for a good mile. I checked my watch and it said 11:00 AM. I threw my right leg over the side of the seat of the bike, looked into my wife's hazel eyes, and said.

"My love, you are the most incredible sexiest woman that God ever created. You get more and more beautiful every day."

Kelly wrapped her arms around my neck and we kissed for a long minute. I looked over her shoulder and said to the dogs.

"Talia, Ronin, you're to guard the family with your lives. Listen to mommy and make sure the kids are doing their homework and chores. And no funny business while mommy and the kids are out of the house. We aren't equipped to have any more doggies in the house. You two are more than enough. Now come here and kiss Daddy."

The two dogs jumped up on my lap wrapped their paws around my shoulders and licked my face. Both of them barked three times which meant they understood their orders. I goosed Kelly on her peach-shaped ass and reminded her that she had the greatest ass ever created. Then I put my finger to my eye and pointed at her, touched my heart, and mouthed. I love you always and forever. A tear ran down her face because she knew in her heart that this assignment might very well be the one that killed me. I started my ride, backed out into the street, and sped off.

Kelly went into the bedroom, and dialed her old team and Face Timed them. She asked for Captain Lennox.

Cap, it's Kelly Volpe. I want back in. Can you get me reinstated and back with the old team? Rick has taken on an incredibly dangerous undercover operation and he's going to need all the help and resources he can get. I already spoke with his boss and he said if you can make it happen it would be great to have us be a part of it. Rick won't know that I'm involved until the operation is concluded."

Captain Lennox told Kelly to raise her right hand and he swore her back into the Suffolk County Police Department and she was back in with her Narcotics team.

Lennox said. "Detective Volpe, we were briefed on this earlier this morning and have started to develop a tactical plan to assist the NYBN. Report to the command tomorrow at 8:00 AM sharp. It's good to have you back. You have permission to bring your K9 dogs in on the op as well. Godspeed Detective and Good Luck."

Jimbo was waiting for me inside Club 40 with Luna the informant. Jeez, he really knew how to pick them. This chick was a stone-cold tweaker and was fiending for another blast of crank, better known as crystal meth. I've seen what that drug can do to a pretty woman or a good-looking man. It destroys their face and fucks up their teeth. They lose a ton of weight and it soaks into their skin leaving a disgusting smell on them. Luna was as skinny as a rail and couldn't stop moving around in the booth that we were sitting in.

I asked Jimbo. "What the hell am I supposed to do with this chick? She can't sit still for a minute. For fuck sake get her something to eat and a soda."

Luna finished her grilled cheese sandwich and her remaining fries and explained that a member of the Excaliburs club who went by the name, Guardrail, slapped her around because she didn't finish him off while she was blowing him. So, now she wanted some payback. I could see that her right eye was badly bruised and her lip was still split in the right corner. She slurped the last bit of soda down.

Luna said, "I can introduce you to one of the Excaliburs through a guy that I screw in the Centurions. They hang out together sometimes at the strip club called The Crystal Cove in Brooklyn. I'll say we know each other from my old job where I was a secretary at a construction company. Plenty of the construction workers ride bikes. We can say you were dropping off parts for their motorcycles."

I said, "Okay, sounds like a plan. But don't go making up any other stuff. It's hard enough to remember one lie. You go expanding on the cover story and you'll fuck us both. Maybe even get us killed."

Luna said, "10-4 Mr. Rick."

Jimbo said, "I'll be tailing you alone tonight. I'll be in my black Malibu. You've got this brother."

At 10:00 PM I picked Luna up at her place and she hopped onto the back of my bike. We arrived at the Crystal Cove at 11:30PM

I scanned the bar checking for the back exit and where the bathrooms were located. I could see a pool table in the far right corner and there were several Excaliburs and Centurions playing pool. In the far left corner was a dart board with a few tables in front of it. The dancing stage was on the right-hand side of the club and there were a few private rooms where the patrons could get lap dances if they paid extra money to the girls.

The chicks that were dancing looked like they came out of a freaking zombie movie. They were all coked up and tweaking out on crank. Two Excaliburs and a member of the Centurions sat at the far end of the dance stage as a boney white skinny chick removed her top to reveal her flat chested breast. She tried to dance seductively in front of them. They laughed with each other and threw a few dollars in her direction. Luna pointed in their direction.

I whispered into her ear, "What the fuck are you doing? You're going to get me killed before this even gets off the ground. Don't point at them for shit's sake. Both of our asses are on the line here. Go get us some beers and take me to the dance stage where they're sitting and introduce me. Just don't go shooting your mouth off. Got me."

She nodded yes and paid the bartender for the beers. The two Excaliburs sitting watching the skinny girl pretending to play with herself were the Sergeant at Arms who went by the name 45 and one of the enforcers named Big Bear. The Centurion was a fully patched member whose club name was Misfit. Luna made the introduction and I stuck my hand out to shake Misfit's hand and then 45's hand.

"Nice to meet you Rick, 45 and Misfit said in unison." Big Bear just said hello and refused to shake my hand. I told Luna to get another round for all of us and then told her to put some money in the jukebox and play some music.

Big Bear asked. "How do you know Luna? That's one crazy bitch."

I said, "I used to deliver bike parts to the construction site where she worked and we became acquainted. Several of the construction workers ride Harleys. I work at a Harley shop in Old Mill Basin. If you guys ever need anything, just stop by and I'll get you what you need."

"That sounds good Rick and it's a pleasure meeting you." 45 said.

The rest of the night I nursed my beers and made sure to spill them out when none of the members of the MCs were looking in my direction. Luna on the other hand was drinking like a fucking fish and trying to score more crank.

I had to get her out of there before she let it out that I was a federal agent. I grabbed her and told her it was time to leave because I had to work in the morning. I said my goodbyes to Big Bear, 45, and Misfit and told them it was a pleasure meeting them. As I got Luna and myself out of the bar I observed one of the Excaliburs who I hadn't been introduced to checking my bike out and writing down my VIN and license plate number and one of the locks had been tampered with on my saddle bag. He'd been rifling through my bags. He quickly turned around and headed back into the bar.

45 said to Big Bear. "I like that guy Rick. He seems like an okay dude."

IV

Alone and Under

Two days later I decided to go to the Crystal Cove on my own. I felt Luna had done enough of an introduction for me to go into the lion's den solo. That's the thing about going under deep. Even though your backup team is in the area. You're still in the belly of the beast all alone. No one has your back while you're engaged in a conversation that could turn extremely ugly in a split second. You can be fighting for your life at the drop of a dime.

I met with Jimbo in the parking lot of the Odd Lot department store. He was driving his Malibu. The backup teams were also there, in an old Ford blue van and a fairly new black Chrysler 300. My bike roared into the lot and I shook hands with the crew. In the van were agents Dylan Peck, Kendrick Poole, and Aiden Reynolds. In the 300 was Paul Howell, who I had personally picked to be involved in the operation, Brock Watkins, and Tatum Beck who if I needed to have as an ol' lady would be introduced in the later stages of the investigation.

Tatum and Kelly were also best friends. Kelly knew she could trust Tatum with my life and she wouldn't try any funny business. Not that I would ever even think about that with any woman. No woman could even come close to my wife. Never have I even thought about cheating on Kelly and neither has she on me. We trusted each other one thousand percent.

I said to the seven members of the team. "Listen up mates. I have a gut feeling this is going to be a real grinder of an investigation. Aiden you're the best writer in the group, can you double-check my work before I submit the FRs (field reports)? Also, are you good with typing them out and handing them into the ASAC and the SAC?" Aiden said, "No problem Rick."

I continued the brief. "We all know those two tight asses upstairs will try and shut us down if we don't have our t's crossed and our i's dotted. So, ghost me the best you can but don't leave my ass out there to get killed. Stay back just far enough that one of the vehicles can see where the fuck I'm at or the place I'm in. If I'm wired, the code words that the shit is going to hit the fan are *(Fucking Now)*. These fucking maniacs are brutal and nasty fuckers.

23

We've got to have our shit as tight as a duck's ass on this one. Jimbo and I have heard through the chain of command that Washington is keeping a close eye on us with this operation. The last thing I want to say. We go big or go home. I'm not looking to make some bullshit small buys of crank or one gun buy. I want a truckload of evidence to put these bastards away for a long time. Let's try and take them all down. Starting with the Brooklyn chapter. Then all the other East Coast chapters. Lastly the Mother Club."

After the instructions were given I started my hog up and rode to the Crystal Cove. I could see a row of about twenty or so bikes parked in front of the Cove. I backed my bike into the far end and left it unlocked. I knew no one could steal it due to the kill switch that Uncle Bobby had installed.

Uncle Bobby had shown me a few tricks on how to fake that the bike took a few attempts to kick over if I needed to use that maneuver. I would need to use a trick or two to catch a few of the OMGs trying to snoop around and see what was inside of them.

Inside I could see several of the Excaliburs and Centurions whose photos were on the whiteboard in the office in Downtown Manhattan. From the Excaliburs were the President, Hatchet, the VP, Whippet, Guardrail, and 45. The Centurion's President, Doberman, and his VP, XXX, and the Sergeant at Arms, Keg were sitting at two tables that had been joined together. There were several other members that I didn't know yet also in the Cove and they were all giving me the 1000-yard prison stare.

I said to myself. "Okay Rickster, keep your cool. You've got this. The first sign of trouble, you already know where both exits are. If the exits are blocked, jump through the side window, and haul your ass the fuck out of there."

I took a seat at the bar. Sitting next to me was a member of the Centurion's Vamp. I introduced myself, "How you doing? I'm Rick Mason, nice place here. Chicks aren't bad looking."

In my mind, I was thinking. "I wouldn't touch these skanks with a ten-foot pole." Vamp said, "What's up? I'm Vamp"

He smiled to show his sharp fangs which a dentist had implanted in his mouth. He said. "These fuckers are sharp as razors and will sink into any person's skin like butter. I also love vampire movies and wanted to be one when I was a kid. Crazy right? It's nice to meet you. What kind of work do you do Rick?"

I told him that I worked at the Harley-Davidson shop in Brooklyn.

Vamp said, "That's cool maybe I'll stop by this week. I need a new set of leather gloves."

I said. "I'll hook you up really good, no worries. I got you. Just come in Monday through Friday between 10:00 AM and 5:00 PM. I'm off on the weekends."

Vamp said." Shit is that a Schott Perfecto leather Jacket you're wearing. That's one hell of a leather. Where did you get that piece?"

I said, "I know a few people in the industry that can pretty much get me whatever I need."

Vamp downed his beer and I bought him another round. After he finished it he took me over to meet a few of the Centurion's. He told them that I worked at the bike shop and could hook them up with whatever they needed at a good price. We had a few more rounds of beers and when no one was looking in my direction I dumped my beer out onto the floor or in a garbage can.

I purchased a few more rounds and we hit it off. The night went smoothly and I could see several of the Excaliburs eyeballing me and sizing me up. That was a good thing. I knew sooner or later Vamp would make an intro to the big boys in the club.

The next few weeks, I was going to the Cove every night and watching several members of the Excaliburs make narcotic sales to the tweakers and coke heads in the bar. I used my photogenic memory to log all the sales of narcotics and which members of the Excaliburs were dealing. I didn't dare wear a wire that early into the investigation.

I was wondering why the Centurions weren't dealing any drugs but later found out that the owner of the Cove was the father of an ol' lady of a patched member of the Excaliburs. So, they had the Cove locked down and were taking 25% percent of the club every night and drinking all the booze and beer for free. I added extortion to the list of charges that the Caliber's had already committed.

So far, in the first month of the investigation, I'd observed several of the members engaged in narcotic sales and being in possession of cocaine, meth, and committing extortion of the owner. The owner had no love for those shitheads. But he knew the consequences he'd suffer if he went to the cops or tried to oppose them. I had been told on one of the previous nights that I was there but had to leave early that a member of the Excaliburs who went by the name, Serpent beat the hell out of a guy who was there on a date with his girlfriend. She'd been flirting with Serpent and the guy told him that she was with him. That was a big mistake on his part and it landed him in the hospital for two weeks. Serpent and another Excalibur named Lizard broke the guy's jaw.

Serpent and Lizard were twins and had several reptiles as pets. They were heavily tattooed and looked like they hadn't bathed for months. Both wore ZZ top beards and had pot bellies. Two greasy mother fuckers that liked to double-team any woman they could get their hands on. Either by consent or force. I'd sent several reports on them and listed the abuse and rape of victims.

I knew that sooner or later I'd have to get some clearance from the US attorney's office to engage in or conduct some felonies to make the investigation stick like gorilla glue. The Excaliburs were a well-organized criminal enterprise and they prided themselves for never being infiltrated by a federal or undercover police organization. That would soon change if I had anything to do about it.

Mid July an Excalibur named Blade walked into the bike shop that was operated by an ex-police officer from the NYPD. He was Uncle Bobby's best friend. Two of the workers in the shop were agents with the NYBN. They wore a mini earpiece in their ears so Uncle Bobby could tell them what parts to give to the customers when they were in the store. I had no use for the earpiece because I already knew every part and every make of a Harley-Davidson. Blade asked for the worker named Rick.

I came out from the back and introduced myself. "I'm Rick, what can I do you for friend?"

I took a long stare at his cut. It was a black leather vest with a top (Rocker) that said Excaliburs in a quarter moon shape. The middle patch was of a skull with wings with two swords that were crossed under the skull head. The bottom rocker read New York and on the left of the skull log was a diamond-shaped patch that read 1%. The right-hand side read MC. There were several other patches on the front of the vest that I had no idea of their meaning yet along with his club name Blade. He had long greasy hair and was sleeved out with tattoos. I could tell the guy did some serious hard time in the joint. He was medium build and had some definition in his arms. He wore rings on all of his fingers that were of skulls and naked women. A real hard-core biker.

"How are you doing, Rick? Vamp told me that you'd hook us up with parts if we needed them"

I said, "Sure thing Blade, it's nice to meet you. I've seen you around in the Cove a lot. That place rocks. What do you need?"

Blade said. "I need some front brake pads dude. And by any chance would you be able to install them for me? I got no mechanic skills when it comes to keeping my bike maintained. I always have someone helping me out with shit."

I went to the back of the shop and made sure the video and audio recording equipment was running. I walked up to the counter with the brake pads and rang him up.

"Okay, Blade that will be $75.00 for parts and I'll have it done in thirty minutes."

Blade smiled and said. "Damn, Vamp wasn't kidding. You really do hook a brother up. I was figuring it was going to run me at least $250 to $300 bucks"

I finished the job in about thirty-five minutes but I was taking my time and studying his bike engine and frame. I noticed the defaced VIN on the right front of the frame near the steering head while I was working on his bike. I knew it was a stolen bike. I checked for the VIN at the base of the rear cylinder on the right side. It was also scratched off. I could only see five numbers which were randomly left there to confuse any law enforcement officer or agent.

That was another charge against the Excaliburs but better yet, a huge advantage for me which I would slowly integrate into the club. I would tell them that I was running a stolen parts and bike operation behind the owner's back. It was my side hustle. I needed to speak with Uncle Bobby ASAP on how to do that. Blade came out of the Dunkin Donuts from across the street as I was gathering up my tools.

Blade asked, " How's it going?"

I said, "All done my friend." Blade asked me. "Hey, Rick, are you going to the Staten Island run this weekend?"

I said, "Man, I'd love to go but I have no one to ride out with and I thought it was by invitation only."

Blade said. "Bud, you can ride with me and the Excaliburs. You'll be my guest and I can introduce you to the other members. They're great guys and they can barbecue the fuck out of ribs and steaks."

I was elated and said, "I'm there Blade, thanks for the invite. Where should I meet you and what time?" He said, "Be at the Cove at 9:00 AM this Friday. We like to go there the day before to set up our tents and gear. Bring some camping equipment like a sleeping bag and warm clothes. It gets freaking cold out in the woods at night."

He started his bike up and sped out onto the street. I used a cellphone that couldn't be traced back to NYBN and called Jim.

He answered on the third ring and said, "Hey Rick, what's cooking, brother?"

I was so pumped and screamed. "Guess who just got invited to the Staten Island run this weekend. That crazy fucker Blade came into the shop and needed his front brake pads changed. I gave him a great deal and did the job myself. Better yet the bike he was riding was stolen. These fuckers are stealing bikes and more than likely selling the parts they aren't using to other clubs or your everyday rider. I can use this to create a cover story where I have a stolen bike and parts operation going on the side. It's another charge bud. I leave for Staten Island on Friday morning. Get the teams out there and have them get a motel twenty or thirty miles away. I don't want them that close during daylight hours."

Jimbo said, "Great job Rick. Can you get downtown ASAP? The ASAC and SAC want a verbal report from you like yesterday."

I said. "Okay, I'll be a good boy scout and be there in an hour barring that there's no traffic on 278 (Brooklyn Expressway)."

I called Kelly and told her the good news and said that we should take the kids out for dinner. Maybe for some Mexican food or Chinese.

I said, "Babe, "I'll be home around 6:30. Have the rugrats ready to roll. And you be prepared for a long night my lady."

Kelly said. "Rick, you're so bad. See you in a few hours. I'll feed the pups and get everyone ready to roll. Can't wait to see you. But before we go you're going to trim your beard and shave your head. right?"

I said, "Yes, dear. But it may be the last time I can actually trim my goatee for a while."

I arrived at the office in just under fifty minutes and took a seat in the SAC's office. The ASAC and Jim were also present. The SAC was Jacob Sharp an agent that had no idea of what was going on when it came to undercover operations. The ASAC Archie Collier had done his fair share of undercover work but had been converted into a yes sir kind of guy. Archie was all about the paperwork and it had to be handed in on time. Especially my FRs (Field Reports) and IRs (Incident Reports) which would be typed up and on his desk within twenty-four hours of any incident.

He turned into a real douchebag. Archie began the meeting by asking me, "So, Rick, where are we with this investigation?"

I said, "Well, sir, I've observed several members of the Excaliburs doing narcotic sales and being in possession of said narcotics. Most of the drugs are cocaine and meth. But I have heard rumblings about the drug fentanyl being dealt also. You know the drug that killed the teenager last week in Manorville Long Island out in Suffolk County."

Archie responded with a wiseass remark. "I know where Manorville is Agent Mason. Please continue."

I wanted to say, "Go fuck yourself. But I continued my report. "I observed two of the main members with guns tucked in their waistbands. Also, they're without a doubt stealing motorcycles and more than likely breaking them down and running a chop shop somewhere. It's another charge to hit them with."

The SAC spoke next. "Agent Mason, how do you know about the stolen bike?"

"I changed out brake pads for an Excalibur who goes by the name Blade. The VIN on the bike had been defaced."

The SAC said, "Okay, I'll need some solid charges on them. I want sales to you by the members of the club. I want you to buy weight when it comes to the narcotic sales and make sure you buy a good amount of the fentanyl. See if you can buy a few guns also. Go to the clerk and get $4000 in cash for buy money. And Rick let's get them on the RICO Act."

(The Racketeer Influenced and Corrupt Organizations Act (RICO) of 1970 seeks to strengthen the legal tools in evidence gathering by establishing new penal prohibitions and providing enhanced sanctions and new remedies for dealing with the unlawful activities of those engaged in organized crime. The law's purpose is to prevent organized crime from infiltrating legitimate businesses that operate in interstate commerce).

Jacob then said, "Take another grand for personal expenses. Make sure to keep receipts and hand them in to your ASAC at the end of the month. Good luck, Agent Mason."

Jimbo and I walked out and back into his office. He said, "Well, that went better than I expected. Let's hit the pavement with both feet and take these bastards down."

I said, "Hold on there, big fella. Listen for this to work I'm going to need clearance from the U.S. Attorney himself and the ASAC to commit some questionable acts. I'm talking about moving drugs across county lines into Manhattan, Jersey, PA, and Boston. Those are the other chapters and the main charter is right here in Manhattan in the heart of Hell's Kitchen on the Westside off of 52nd Street. I'll more than likely be in possession of illegal firearms, engaging in assaults, and transporting drugs for them. That's the situation here. I'll need to become one of them if and when I'm asked to become a prospect.

I've already passed the hang-around stage. Next will be the invite to become a prospect and I know just the way to do it. I can make it happen during the Staten Island run. It'll mean me getting into a brawl or helping one of the Excaliburs out in a fight they pick. You can be damn sure that will happen during this weekend. I've seen them do it several times already at the Cove. But not to the extent of being vicious. I can tell it's coming full force with several of those lowlife fuckers. Jimbo, you need to get me the clearance on this. I need to know I won't be charged by the U.S. Attorney down the road after this investigation is completed. We both know how ambitious an AUSA can be if it means he or she will move up the ladder in their office."

Jim thought about it for a few minutes and made the call. He recorded the conversation. He'd advised the AUSA he was doing so. The assistant U.S. attorney who would be handling the case was Bryce Cobb a sharp lawyer who was one of the best in the U.S. Attorney's in the Eastern District. After forty minutes of getting all the clearances from the NY, D.C. offices, and the U.S. Attorney it was all systems go on operation King Arthur.

V

The Test

Kelly and I decided to bring the kids into the city to a Japanese Hibachi restaurant. We ordered the surf and turf special. Shrimp and steak with vegetables and extra rice for me. The kids were entertained by the chef throwing the egg in the air and catching it in his chef hat then tossing the egg high towards the ceiling and breaking it as it came down to the table with his spatula. He made a volcano out of the onions and finished his show by twirling his cooking utensils in both hands. I could tell he was an expert with edged weapons. The meal was incredible and the kids had a great time. That night was a night to remember with Kelly and we held onto each other all through the night and into the morning.

I said to her, "I'll make the kids breakfast and send them off to school. Stay in bed and I'll be up to give you breakfast in bed."

I crept up the stairs with Kelly's waffles and a slice of homemade peach cobbler pie. She finished her food and smiled at me. Her white teeth sparkled and her eyes lit up the room.

She said, "You're the best cook in the world. Do you know that?" I laughed and said, "Are you trying to seduce me before I go to work beautiful?"

She put the folding tray on the floor and I jump into bed with her. We had passionate sex and then showered together. I raced over to meet Jimbo at the Odd Lot parking lot before I headed to the Cove to meet up with Blade and the other Excaliburs that would be riding out with us. My heart was pounding as I pulled into the front of the Cove. I backed my ride at the end of the line of other bikes. There were sixteen Harley-Davidsons parked along the curb and I could hear voices inside the Crystal Cove. They were screaming the way a team does before a big game. It sounded like the Excaliburs were gearing up for a battle against a rival bike club.

I quickly checked around the rear of the Cove. There was a black van parked in the back and I observed a patched member who went by the name Jason loading an open box of handguns and handheld axes into the back of the van. He threw a blanket over them and made several more trips in and out of the back of the Cove to load the club's camping gear, frozen meat, cases of beer, whiskey, and charcoal for the grills. I went back out to the front and waited for Blade to exit the Cove and introduce me to the rest of the members whom I wasn't familiar with. Blade made the introductions and the Road Captain Guardrail gave the details of the ride to us. Which roads and highways we'd be traveling on. The van with the weapons would be driving in the rear of the formation. During actual time on the road or at intermediate stops during the run, Guardrail was the ranking club officer, deferring only to the President or Vice President. The Road Captain has overall authority on a club ride.

I was instructed by Whippet the VP to ride in the back of the club and keep my formation tight and not cause the members whom I was either riding next to or behind to crash. If that were to occur, I'd be killed on site. When I was told this, a knot formed inside my stomach and I knew from then on that if I were to become a prospect, I would be venturing into the heart of darkness and complete evil. There was no turning back for me now. I was going into the pit of hell. It would take everything inside my soul and body to return to my wife and children as the husband and father who had just left them only hours beforehand. The ride lasted close to an hour and a half. We'd stopped at two gas stations to top off our gas tanks, hydrate, and eat some junk food.

I kept thinking to myself. "Rick, if you don't watch what the hell you're eating you'll be heading down a slippery slope of obesity."

I prided myself on being in good shape and keeping my body like a piece of steel. I made a vow to make sure to keep doing calisthenics every morning, no matter what the situation was at hand. Several of the Excaliburs were in decent shape but most were just fat disgusting vile human beings.

Guardrail put his right hand up and did a circle motion in the air to let us know to mount up and hit the road. Several of the Excaliburs were looking at me from head to toe. Eye fucking me like they wanted to beat the living shit out of me. I kind of thought it was comical but also very scary. I knew if one of those bastards were to pick a fight with me, I'd be fighting all of them. They didn't fight one on one unless they were inside the pit. (The pit I would later find out was a circle of club members that surrounded two men that were going to fight hand to hand either over a beef they had with each other or just some good old letting-off steam bullshit). I knew I would be inside the pit in no time. We made it to Staten Island and the officers of the club picked out the areas they wanted to set up their camps in. I chose a small area with a nice oak tree that faced the entire club. I wasn't going to give any of them a chance to come up from behind me while I was resting or sleeping.

Blade approached me and said, " Now listen to me carefully, Rick. Don't go asking anyone any questions about the club or club business. Just hang close to me and my ol' lady Shelly."

As he was talking with me he took some white powder out of a folded piece of tinfoil and placed some of it on the top of his hand between his thumb and first finger. He snorted it up and the pupils of his eyes widened.

He said, "Bro, this is some good fucking crank. It will keep you up all night and day. You want a hit, man?"

I said, "No not yet, Blade. Maybe in a little while. I'm just taking all of this in. This is the life man. Free living, women, beer, food, and plenty of camaraderie. Man, I feel like I belong here. Thanks for asking me to ride out with you and your club."

Blade said, "Rick if you're still feeling that way after the weekend. I'll put in a good word for you with Hatchet and we'll see about you maybe becoming a prospect for the club. But just be cool and get to know the guys for the next few days. Oh, and one more thing. Don't ever hit on any of the member's ol' ladies. That's a fucking death sentence for you. For now, stay clear of Mamas and Sweet Butts. If you want to you can hang and fuck the House Mouses. They're the ones looking for a walk on the wild side. You'll know the difference bud."

I just nodded toward him. I couldn't give a shit about any of the chicks on the grounds. Other clubs were starting to roll into the camp area and took their respective areas. Then The Guardians rode into the campground and the Excaliburs all lined up and took ready positions in case something jumped off between the two clubs. The Caliburs held their hatchets at their sides behind their legs. My stomach tightened as I stood in the back of the club ready to fight their sworn enemies. Then I saw a familiar face from my past and I almost shit myself.

"I whispered to myself, "Keep cool and don't fucking make any hand gestures or make eye contact with him."

The mother chapter of the Excaliburs rode into the grounds around 10:00 PM and that's when I met that piece of shit, Ripper the Mother Chapter's Sergeant at Arms. He had his arms around two vial-looking skanks that were tweaked out of their minds. He kept pawing at them and sticking his fingers inside them like they were jelly donuts. Our eyes made the first initial contact and that was it. He was like a raving fucking lunatic. He strolled over to me with his big, barreled chest and heavily tatted arms and said.

"What in fucks name are you looking at dick head. You keep eyeballing me and I'll fucking skull fuck you to death. You worthless piece of shit. Get the fuck out of my area."

I figured it was do or die, there was no backing down from this psychotic tweaked-out lunatic. I said, "How you doing? I'm Rick Mason and I'm here as a guest of Blade."

Ripped spat as he spoke, "I don't give a fuck whose guest you are. I don't like the way you look. I think you're a cop."

He then spat on my leather boots with a wad of tobacco juice from his mouth. The smell of it almost made me vomit. I knew he was going to be my biggest ball buster if I was to prospect.

I thought to myself, "Bring it on mother fucker. Dealing with you will be like taking candy from a baby."

One of the last MCs to ride in was the Centurions. I recognized all of them from the whiteboard in the Manhattan office. Vamp walked over to me and greeted me with a big hug and said, "How the fuck are you doing Rick? It's been a minute. Listen I got some good shit so come on over later and we'll do a few blasts and get fucked up. I'll introduce you to the rest of the club tonight."

"Sounds like a plan Vamp. Talk to you later. How's the new tires holding up?" Vamp, said, Man, you're a Magician bro. Thanks again for hooking me up last week."

He turned and left to hang out with his club. The one good thing that had just been established was that Vamp had recognized me as a brother and not a hang-around. That would prove to be huge during the three-day weekend. I could see Ripper speaking with the Brooklyn chapter's president Hatchet. He was pointing in my direction. I just sat against the tree that I'd picked out to camp near and nursed a beer. A few minutes later Hatchet and Whippet of the Brooklyn chapter came over to me and told me to stand up.

Hatchet spoke first and said, "So, Rick, Blade says you're okay people. What's your story friend? Why did you want to ride with us this weekend?"

I said, I love riding my Harley and I know my way around bikes and figured if anyone needs a hand with their bikes this weekend I could help them out. I'm all about making new friends. I came home from overseas several years back and I'm having some difficulty fitting back into the world. I'd say society but fuck that. I'm all about being free and doing whatever the fuck I want. Good or bad."

Whippet spoke next, "You know the war is over and all that crazy shit that happened over there. You're home now and safe."

He then showed his Death Before Dishonor tattoo from the Marines. He said, "I was a Machine Gunner. What branch did you serve in Rick?"

Fuck, the moment of truth had come. I knew I couldn't give them too much information. Jimbo hadn't made any calls to have a new record for me put into the system. I also needed to call in a few favors at the Pentagon to make a few things happen.

"I was an Army Ranger and saw some action in the Middle East," I told them I was a sniper.

Hatchet asked, "How many people have you killed?"

I grinned, "Let's just say, I killed a lot of bad guys over there protecting the Marines and Army infantries on the ground."

Whippet said, "Well if the club takes a liking to you then we're going to find out all about you Rick."

Hatchet said, "Now, let's get some grub. Rick sit at my table with my wife Sophia and me."

I said, "I'd be honored, Hatchet."

The ribs and steaks were unbelievable. Blade wasn't joking. These lowlife criminals could barbecue like five-star chefs. What a waste of talent. The two Excaliburs on the grill were the enforcer named Jason, and Treasurer Riddler. I wanted to go up to them and slap both of them on the back of the head and tell them they could be cooking in any five-star restaurant and be making a tremendous living legally. I made sure to have seconds and thirds on the meat and didn't eat the salads or potatoes. It was all protein that I took in.

After we ate I helped clean up the area with the two prospects. The Caliburs were hazing the hell out of them and running the poor bastards into the ground. My first test came around 10:30 PM. I was sitting at a picnic table with Hatchet, and Big Bear just shooting the shit when that crazy fucker, Ripper came over to the table.

Ripper slurred, "So, I see you've gotten on the good side of Hatchet here. Well, Mr. President you just make sure this mother fucker is no cop. Because I'm banking on it, that he's the fuzz. And if he is and any of us go down. You're going to be the first mother fucker under my blade, then I'll cut this cop's head off along with his entire family's heads. You got that, Hatchet? Now let's do some lines with your new pet project."

Hatchet fired back, "Hey, Ripper, just relax your half retarded brain and chill the fuck out. The weekend just started and your starting bull shit already. I'll set out some lines and we'll all have a snort. Even the new guy here will do a line to prove he's not a cop. Cops can't do drugs, even if they're working undercover."

Test number one had come and it was do or die. My cover team was a good ten miles out as per my suggestion. They could never reach me if the shit hit the fan. I was on my own and now it was time to go to work. I'd been in these types of situations before and had a quick hand and skillful way of making it look like I was snorting the narcotics when told to do so. The only problem was that I wasn't doing the crank off my hand, it was being set out in lines on the picnic bench. My heart was starting to race and I needed to slow it down or I would be made for an undercover for sure.

Hatchet snorted a huge line into his nose, then whippet. Ripper snorted a line the size of a cigarette. It was now my turn. I asked Hatchet if I could borrow his straw to stall a few seconds longer.

He said, "Dude, just roll up a bill and hit that shit already."

I rolled a five-dollar bill and put it next to the white powder line on the table then close to my nostril, I stalled for another moment and got ready to do my magic trick of making the line disappear. Only thing was, I'd never done it this way and had no idea if I'd be able to pull the stunt off. Just then a scream came from the other end of our camp. The three of them turned to see what the commotion was. I swept the drugs off the table and snorted loudly. Then held my fingers to my nose pretending to have snorted the line.

I screamed out, "Fuck yeah that's some good fucking shit."

I kicked some dirt over the white substance on the ground and was in the clear. The commotion was that one of the ol' ladies was pregnant and the other club members were celebrating. Saved by the bell. A few minutes later I asked to speak with Hatchet alone and out of earshot.

I told Hatchet, "I've got to keep a low profile with the drugs man. I'm on parole and don't want to get violated. I get tested every two weeks. It's gonna take a lot of Golden Seal to get this shit out of my system. I don't want to get busted by my parole officer."

Hatchet said, "I got you, bro, It's cool man. You passed that test with flying colors. You're clear, not to do any of that shit if you don't want to."

VI

Throwing Down

By Saturday afternoon the booze was getting downed by hundreds of bikers and the drugs were being handed out like candy. I'd observed over forty narcotic transactions between Excaliburs and the Centurions. They were dealing to the other clubs that they were on good terms with and other campers that were looking to score stuff. One disturbing thing I'd heard was a conversation between the Vice President of the Centurions, XXX, and an Excalibur, Mohawk planning on giving some of the teenage girls that were hanging out with the clubs some ecstasy and fentanyl. They said they'd wait for the girls to be totally blitzed and rape them. I knew I'd have to keep a close watch on those two scumbags to keep it from happening.

At 9:00 PM I slipped away to update Jimbo on the incidents of the day. That I'd committed to memory and the players that were involved in the narcotic transactions. I found an area that had plenty of evergreen trees near one of the restrooms. I sent Jimbo a long text message then deleted it. Just in case one of the Caliburs wanted to check my phone to see who I'd been speaking or texting with. As I started to walk away I heard a voice from the past whisper a name I hadn't gone by in many years.

"Rogue, is that you brother?"

It was my old team leader from Seal Team Six, Leo Steele (Kahuna). He was wearing a Guardians leather vest and on the right front pocket, there was a skinny rectangular patch that read Vice President and another one under it read, Kahuna.

He said, "What in fucks name are doing here, and why are you in the Excalibur camp. Do they know who you are?"

I grabbed him by his arm, pulled him behind a big tree, and said. "Hey brother, it's great to see you, and no they don't know who the fuck I am. I'm on a case. You need to stay clear of me and don't blow my cover. Is your number the same? I'll have Uncle Bobby call you and update you on everything. You, me, and the Guardians need to work together on this or I promise you, the Excaliburs and the Guardians will go to war."

39

Kahuna said, "Alright, Rogue, the Guardians are at your disposal. You know we're not into that criminal shit. We do some high-level security and on occasion, grab a bad guy for a few bail bondsmen. A few of us do some mercenary operations for you know who. But we're one-percenters to the hilt and we don't fuck around. We have ties to the predominant MCs that do shady shit but never around us. We do favors for each other at times. But the Excaliburs are fucking bad news for all the MCs. Those lowlife are the evilest bastards we've ever seen. Be careful and keep your eyes open at all times. Give Kelly and the kids a kiss for me. Godspeed brother, Hooah."

I said, "I will. I'll be in touch through Uncle Bobby. Stay frosty, brother. Keep your phone on at all times."

We looked around and made sure no other clubs had observed us speaking together and we parted ways. I didn't know if that had complicated the mission or if it'd helped. I would soon find out. As I was walking away I observed another club setting up their camp about fifty yards from the Caliber's camp. It was one of the Caliburs enemies. The Marquis are into some heavy gun running, narcotics trafficking, and dog fighting. I could tell something was brewing; several of them were pointing toward the Excaliburs campsite. I needed to head back to alert them.

Late Sunday afternoon many of the clubs had dispersed and went their separate ways. The only ones left were the Centurions and the Marquis. The Guardians were packed up and getting ready to roll out. Hatchet and 45 gazed sternly at the Guardians as they rode away through the densely wooded pines. Ripper and the Mother Club had left several hours earlier and all that was left of the Excaliburs were the Brooklyn chapter, two prospects, and myself.

One of the Marquis yelled at Hatchet, "What the fuck are you looking at scumbag?"

I walked next to Whippet and Riddler the treasurer and said to them, "If they make a move I got your six all the way. I've been waiting to let my hands fly for a few years."

They looked at each other and grinned as if to say, "We got us a real banger."

45 said to the Marquis President, "You have some kind of beef with us bro."

The Marquis President said, "We ain't your fucking brothers so if we're going to do this, let's get to it."

Big Bear said, "Enough talk."

There were ten Excaliburs, two prospects, and myself against fourteen Marquis. Three Marquis went right for Hatchet so I quickly went by his side. The first guy tried to sucker punch him and I slid in front of Hatchet and blocked the guy's roundhouse punch with my forearm. His forearm shattered. He went to his knees holding his arm. I sent a front kick into his solo plex and he went down for the count. Hatchet had engaged in a fight with one of the other guys and the third Marquis was getting ready to hit him with a haymaker from behind.

I went in the direction of the punch, tucked my chin into my upper chest, and stepped into the punch, and it landed right where I wanted it to. Into the top of my forehead. The guy screamed in pain. His hand broke instantly. I sent my left elbow into the left side of his jaw then I grabbed the back of his neck and whipped him into a half circle and stood him back up again and sent my right forearm across the bridge of his nose and head. He flipped backward into the air and was knocked out. His nose was broken badly. The other Marquis had witnessed my fighting skills and the president called a halt to the fight. They grabbed the two guys that I'd knocked out and they scattered back to their camp and fled the grounds.

Hatchet and the other members of the clubs looked at me and were speechless. Then Blade said, "Who and what the fuck are you dude? That was some Steven Segal shit and Bruce fucking Lee Kung Fu shit. Who taught you how to fight like that man? I want to learn how to do that crazy shit. You've got some badass fighting skills, bro."

I said, "First of all, I'm just a guy. A nobody looking for my way in life. Secondly, I was trained in the arts at a young age. My Uncle sent me to the best fighting schools in Chinatown and on the Island. I even spent two years learning Aki Ju Jitsu in Japan. I'm a black belt in Kung Fu and 4th Dan in Aki Ju-Jitsu. When I saw your president about to be attacked I just went into fighting mode. I figured it was the least I could do for you guys in return for showing me such a kick-ass weekend."

Hatchet said, "I vote right now that Rick here, becomes a prospect for the club. I'll be his sponsor. All in favor raise your hand."

All of the Excaliburs raised their hands and told me to be at the clubhouse the following Thursday and I would get my leather vest and my bottom rocker, which read Prospect.

The two members of the Centurions and Excaliburs who were planning on rapping the teenage girls had been warned by Whippet and Big Bear not to draw any negative attention to the club out in the open. I would later discover during a night out of drinking at the Cove how brutal these bastards really were. A lot of the Excaliburs were stone-cold killers and rapists and would fuck anything they could hold down. I would soon witness how terribly they treated their women. I should say any woman that they crossed paths with that they thought they could molest and screw.

I rode with the club back to Brooklyn and once we hit the Belt Parkway we parted ways. Hatchet had given me instructions to be back at the clubhouse in Marine Park on Thursday and be ready to be given a detailed background check by the club's private eye, who was an ex-cop. I had my work cut out for me and so did my team. I needed to develop a background story and start backstopping my new identity.

(Backstopping is the process of establishing and maintaining documentation and facilitating the support of covert identities and structures capable of withstanding scrutiny.) This operation would require the highest level of covert backstopping for me to perform my role as the undercover. I would need a new driver's license, a new mailing address, and all my bike and vehicle registrations and insurance cards would need to be put into Rick Mason's name. I needed junk mail in my undercover name and a lease for a rental house in Brooklyn. I felt it would be better if I lived in one of the towns there

All of this would need to be set up within the next three days. Criminal records, a parole record, and an officer that we could trust to say, he was my P.O. High school records. I needed to call my old guidance counselor to have my name switched from Volpe to Mason on my yearbook photo. Old neighbors who of course would be undercovers portraying to be them. Lastly, I had to call General Walton at the Pentagon. I dialed his number and asked for extension 503. A raspy voice on the other end answered right away.

"This is General Walton, whom am I speaking with."

"General, this is Rick Volpe. How are you doing sir?"

"Rick, it's good to hear your voice. How the hell are you and the family holding up?"

"All good sir, I need a huge favor from you. I'm working on a very covert operation for the NYBN. I'm deep undercover and I need my military records to be altered from Rick Volpe to Rick Mason. Just the last name. Keep my first name as it is. This includes every medal and operation I ever performed in the Rangers and the Seals. It must be by Rick Mason. My war record, all my kills have to have been accomplished by Rick Mason. Even when I was caught behind enemy lines and captured. Make sure to include every medal I received. Can you make it happen?"

"Rick, that's a tall order, but consider it done. You're the best damn soldier the Army and Navy ever had. Just know that your country may call upon you one day in return for this favor. Are you good with that, Lieutenant Volpe?"

"Yes, sir, General Walton."

VII

Prospect

By midweek things had pretty much come together with what needed to be done concerning my new background. Many of the things had already been in place from the prior investigation with the white supremacist group. Jimbo and I were sure that the Excaliburs would leave no stone unturned. I'd been given the heads up by a member of the Centurions, Misfit, on who the Excaliburs private eye was. He was a retired NYPD first-grade detective and very sharp. Misfit was grateful for a favor I had done for him the prior week. Uncle Bobby had done a masterpiece of artwork on his gas tank. I ran a check on the private eye who was Hank Hutchinson. The guy knew his craft and was an expert at finding holes in backstopping. But he'd need to dive extremely deep to uncover my background. And the powers to be at the U.S. Attorney's office and the NYBN weren't going to let that happen. Operation King Arthur was becoming a huge case for all involved.

Kelly had told me that she'd be running around doing so many things that she'd be sending the kids to her mother and sister's house for the rest of the summer. They'd be back the week before Labor Day. I told her I'd take her out to our favorite Mexican restaurant so we could eat together before I started to prospect. I knew that prospecting would require me to be at the clubs beckoning 24 hours a day.

Kelly reported to her office at the 7th precinct in Suffolk County. The NYBN and her group had formed a task force and would be keeping it on the down low when it came to the undercover operation. Many of the members had run-ins or had been conducting some type of investigation on the Excaliburs. They agreed to put all of their investigations together and have them go federal. The members of the task force including Kelly were all sworn in as U.S Deputies of the Marshal Service. The task force included two Marshals, two ATF, several DEA agents, and the Suffolk County Narcotics unit.

The NYBN would take the lead on the operations and all the task force personnel involved. They kept me in the dark when it pertained to Kelly's involvement. Kelly was permitted to bring in our dogs Talia and Ronin as the unit's K9s. Her heart was pounding as the whiteboard was revealed and she observed all of the horrendous murders, assaults, and rapes the Excaliburs had been accused of.

44

Meanwhile back in Manhattan where the main unit was operating, Jimbo and I had to report to the SAC's office to brief the brass. I also needed to ask for a voucher of ten thousand dollars for buy money. Bryce Cobb the U.S. Attorney had rented me a house in Sheepshead Bay Brooklyn. The entire house was wired for sound and audio.

The techs did an incredible job of hiding the wires and installing audio and video cameras and ultrasonic jammers just in case the Excaliburs checked for listening and recording devices. There was a secret recording room hidden in one of the walls and it needed a special code to be punched in to gain access. Anytime I had members in the house I would press a code into the TV remote and the equipment would be activated. The walls were soundproofed just in case one of the taping devices stopped. They installed the same equipment into my AMX for when I would need to drive instead of riding my bike.

That night Kelly and I enjoyed the dinner and discussed the plan of attack for me. I could see in her eyes and hear the cracking of her voice that she knew more about the Excaliburs than she led onto. I let it go and just figured she'd made more calls into her old unit to do some further digging into the club.

I asked her. "Is there something you want to tell me about the operation that I don't already know Hun? Because if you know something that I may not, then please tell me."

She said, "Yes, there is. I did some more intelligence work on this and I can tell you one thing for sure. These bastards have been involved in several murders over narcotic deals that have gone bad and have killed innocent people who were just in the wrong place at the wrong time at that strip joint they call home. They're freaking animals and will kill you if they discover that you're a federal agent, Rick. This is no ordinary case. It could kill you. I can't stand the idea of losing you or you going dark on me. Promise me, right here and now, that you'll come home to me and the kids alive and as Rick Volpe. The man I love so deeply and the father that our kids cherish and love."

I said, "I promise sweetheart. I'll bring these bastards down and will come home as Rick Volpe. Someone has to stop them and it might as well be me."

I kissed her on the neck and lips and whispered into her ear. "Love Never To End Beautiful."

We fell asleep in each other's arms. Morning came and we trained together and took the dogs for a nice run. Then Kelly made my favorite breakfast of waffles, eggs, and a stack of bacon. I drank plenty of coffee and then she walked me out to the garage. We looked into each other's eyes for several minutes then I kissed my wife goodbye. I had no idea of what lay ahead of me. But I knew it was going to be a path of violence and insanity.

I rode out to Uncle Bobby's shop and had lunch with him. We shared a few shots of whiskey and he began to tell me what to expect as a prospect. We spoke for over four hours. When the conversation was through Uncle Bobby gave my bike an in depth check. He changed out my spark plugs and put a new air filter on. Then he handed me several boxes of spark plugs, tire repair kits, and cable kits that I would need to help other members change out during long rides.

Uncle Bobby said. "Rick, I've set the table for you when it comes to being a prospect and you know all there is to know about Harleys. Keep your eyes open and try to stay cool at all times. Be safe, son, and know you have plenty of backup out here if you need it. I'll be in the shop with my earpiece on if you need to contact me. Ride safe. I always got your six always."

I pulled into the Marine Park location where the Brooklyn Chapters clubhouse was around 7:00 pm. The other members were already there and inside. The two prospects who thought they were close to possibly finishing their time prospecting were in front on guard duty. Their names were Billy and Brian. They were blood brothers and real dirtbags.

I'd heard through the grapevine from Jason that they weren't Excalibur material and would be shown the door in the coming weeks. I kept that information to myself. Those poor bastards had been put through hell, and for what?" To be told you're out. I was hoping that they would still be around for some of my prospecting to share the duties of the club's bullshit hazing.

Hatchet called me into the room where the club had been holding what is called Church. (Church is a meeting where patched members discuss club business and vote on any changes or in general anything about the club. Prospects typically watch the bikes and do security on the outside during church. At the end prospects are brought in and told anything they need to know about the prior meeting).

He said, "Take a seat, Rick. Are you sure you want in, as a prospect? I'll tell you this. It won't be easy and I'm going to ride your ass personally. Being that I'm going to be your sponsor."

I could see the prospect patch lying on the black leather vest on the table in front of Hatchet. I said, "I'm all in Hatchet, one hundred percent."

45 said, "No brother, you're on your way to becoming a one percenter, baby."

Riddler slid a small hand guide at me and said, "That booklet has all the rules and regulations and bylaws of the club. Along with our motto. You'll be tested on them periodically. So, start studying after the party. You have twenty minutes to sew that patch on, prospect. Welcome to the club, Rick. Don't let us down."

Big Bear said, "Fuck man, the way this dude fights I see him being patched in quicker than any of us ever were. Now let's get to drinking and fucking the mammas out there."

I sewed the patch on within twelve minutes perfectly. I'd been medically trained in sewing wounds in the military and the NYBN special response team. So, it came in handy with the regular sewing of my clothes. If called upon, I could do a surprisingly good job of sewing wounds up in the field. It would later come in handy during this investigation. I walked into the bar area of the club and was congratulated on becoming a prospect by the other members of the Brooklyn chapter and several other East Coast chapter members. They'd come in for the party. I could see Ripper giving me that prison yard stare that he more than likely gave other inmates while serving time.

Ripper called, "Hey Prospect get your ass over here right now." I quickly walked over to him and he got right into my face. "I know you're a cop and when I get you dirty I'm going to kill you and kill your fucking family. Now go get me a fucking beer, maggot."

He then sent a crushing blow into my midsection. I had been ready for it and tightened up and took the punch. I let out the air to let the pain escape my body. Ripper looked disturbed that I didn't double over in pain and said,

"Oh, you're some kind of badass that likes pain huh? Well, mother fucker, I'm going to be your house of pain until you quit or I catch you being dirty."

I went to the bar and grabbed two Budweiser's out of the ice bucket and gave them to him and said. "If you need anything else, Ripper? Just let me know and I'll get it for you right away."

With that, I went about my prospect duties for the night. I was quite sure that fuck had cracked one of one of my ribs on the front of my ribcage. I was having trouble breathing but there was no way I was going to turn back now.

I was in. All I kept thinking was "You cocksuckers are all going down and will never see the light of day if I have anything to do about it."

The night ended around 4:00 AM and I was told to go home and be ready for the weekend. Hatchet said, "Hey prospect, just know we're diving deep into your background and history. So, if you've got any skeletons in your closet. Come clean with me now so I can smooth things out for you before they're discovered by our private investigator. He's very sharp and will find out everything there is to know about you."

I said, "No worries Pres, I'm clean."

The next Saturday afternoon Hatchet and Whippet called me to report to the clubhouse. I pulled into the front of the clubhouse and only saw the officers of the club's bikes outside. I said to myself, "Fuck me, they found out something. What did we forget to change?"

The officers were all hanging around and shooting the shit and stopped what they were doing when I walked inside.

Hatchet spoke first. "I thought I asked you if you had any skeletons in your closet."

I said, "I don't Hatchet. I'm clean and ready to roll with the club."

Whippet said, "Why the fuck didn't you tell us that you were in the Rangers and the Seals. You're a fucking war hero, man. Our guy spoke to someone at the Pentagon and he gave him your service jacket and then the investigator gave it to Hatchet. For fuck sake brother, multiple kills and 99 successful missions completed. You're one bad Hombre dude. Now if you wouldn't mind taking off your vest and shirt."

I said, "Sorry, Whippet, I can't lay down my colors for anyone. It's against club rules."

Hatchet said, "Prospect, this isn't a test. We just want to see it for real if what we read about you is on the up and up."

I removed my vest and tee shirt and they looked at all the scars and bullet holes on my back, chest, and abdomen. Then they took a closer look at the Ranger and Navy Seal Tattoos on my back and chest. 45 had seen enough and so did the others.

45 said, "Get dressed prospect, and thank you for your service. We may be criminals and mother fuckers but we respect the men who fought in our wars. You're one bad mother, bro. I ain't giving you no shit on my end. I'd vote you to be patched in today if I could."

The other members clapped and shook my hand and we drank the rest of the day and night. Chicks and other members came in with a few of the Centurions that had been invited. The officers didn't reveal my service record to anyone, not even the mother club or the other patched members. Hatchet would send my info over to Arthur later that week. He just wanted the president of the Mother Chapter to know that the Brooklyn Chapter very well might have the best prospect to come through in an extraordinarily long time.

VIII

Murders at the Cove

During the following months, I observed and reported the details of countless narcotic transactions between members from the Excaliburs to patrons who frequented Crystal Cove. The dancers were regular customers of the drug dealing that the Excaliburs were engaged in. I had kept watch of Guardrail, 45, Serpent, Blade, and Steel selling tons of crank, coke, and fentanyl. I would always hear 45 telling the tweakers to be extra careful when using the fentanyl.

Then the biggest break in the investigation fell into my lap. All the drug transactions were incredible and damning evidence in the case, but I needed a major violent felony to get them on a RICO Act.

February 1, 2022, I was hanging out with Blade, Lizard, Steel, and Mohawk. They were all high as kites and very loose-lipped about the doings of the club. That particular night I had a recording device on me which was inside a zippo lighter. I kept it on me occasionally to light the patch member's cigarettes. It had a twelve-hour lifespan to record my conversations. I wasn't a big fan of wearing wires during the investigation. If I ever was caught wearing one I'd be killed instantly. I was sitting across from Steel and he moved his head in a way to motion me to come closer to him as he whispered something that had occurred at the Cove a year ago. The other members were throwing darts and playing pool.

Steel whispered, "Hey brother, we fucked up really bad and the club has some heat on us. You heard about that chick last year dying in Manorville from an overdose?"

I played stupid and said, "No man I hadn't heard about that. I don't watch the news or read the newspaper. Forget about me with computers. I have ten thumbs."

Steel said in an exceptionally low voice, "Dude, she was in here that night dancing on the stage trying to get a job as a pole dancer. Chick was smoking crack and doing crank. The boys decided to run a train on her. You know we took turns fucking that tight little pussy for hours. Shit man, we took all of her holes sometimes three of us at one time. Fucking bitch loved it. She kept asking for more blow and wanted to take a little snort of fentanyl. I gave her a hit off my thumbnail.

50

When it was Guardrail's turn to fuck her, she was riding high and fucking him like a bronco. Then she just keeled the fuck over and fell off the pool table.

Her head hit the ground and split open like a ripe pumpkin. We all fucking panicked and Jason and Big Bear threw her in the back of the van and drove her dead ass out into the woods in Manorville. Shit was fucked up. Listen man if I got to do a person I can kill them at the drop of a dime. But that shit just isn't sitting well with me. She was probably 16 at best. Maybe I gave her too much of a hit of fentanyl"

I thought to myself, "Yeah, but you didn't mind raping and sodomizing the young girl, you sick mother fucker." I just wanted to be the judge and executioner right there on the spot.

I said, "Bro, that's some heavy shit man. Keep that on the down low and keep it to yourself. What do you think, we call it a night and sleep this shit off?"

"Yeah, Prospect let's get the fuck out of here and I'll see you tomorrow at the clubhouse. Forget everything I said tonight. Don't ever mention it again or I promise, I'll fucking kill your ass."

I said, "I have no idea what you're talking about. I wasn't even here tonight. I was at home banging my ol' lady all night."

I gunned my bike out of the parking lot and headed to the Odd Lot department store to meet up with Jimbo and the team. They had heard the entire conversation as well from their listening devices.

Jimbo said, "We got them now on a RICO Act. Great job brother. We'll squeeze Steel to give up every bastard that participated in the gang rape. There's no way she would have been willing to engage in intercourse with those vile pigs. We fucking got them now. Listen, that girl they killed was the niece of a member of the Guardians. War is coming and we need to step this investigation up and get as many drug transactions completed quickly. Start to buy weight this week. That's coming from downtown. They're looking to shut us down. I'll be in touch."

I said, "Jimbo, I'm not feeling good about wearing a wire on the 4th of July. It's my first mandatory run and I'm going to be searched and vetted constantly by any member that wants to check me out. That includes the Mother Club. If I get through the first mandatory I'll only have one more left. I'm close to getting patched in, I can feel it. The club is starting to show trust in me more and more.

I'm getting more responsibilities. I have to do a cocaine run this Thursday. I'll be traveling on my hog to the New Jersey Chapter."

Agent Peck said, "Rick, be careful, this shit is getting really dangerous. Keep it together we've got your back."

"Thanks guys, I'll check in with you tomorrow. Just remember I won't be wearing any wire this weekend so ghost me but keep your distance. We don't want them to know the feds are in the area.

Thursday came and Riddler and Serpent handed me two brick packages of cocaine. Riddler said, Don't fuck this up, and make sure you get to the Trenton clubhouse by 2:00 PM."

I said, "No worries Riddler. I'll get it there and call you when I arrive and leave their clubhouse."

Serpent said, "Stay alert and ride safe bro."

It was 11:30 AM. I had two and a half hours to get to Trenton, New Jersey. I made sure that I wasn't being tailed and met up with Team One and Aiden Reynolds field-tested the coke and took several photos of the two bricks which were two kilos of 95% pure cocaine. He rewrapped it and sealed it like it had been before he tested it.

Agent Reynolds said, "Alright brother, you better haul your ass out of here. We'll be right behind you in case you get pulled over."

I said, "Just keep checking your rearview mirrors and make sure no one is tailing you or me."

I hit I-95 and arrived with twenty minutes to spare. I backed my ride into the front of their clubhouse and was greeted by their President, Brooks who asked me, "Hey Prospect, you have the stuff?"

"Sure, thing Pres, it's in my saddlebags. I'll get them out."

Brooks shouted, "Don't you fucking touch it. It's our product and I want to make sure you're not wired and your bike is clean. Stand the fuck up Prospect and strip down naked right fucking now."

I removed my boots and banged them out on the gravel. Then I took the rest of my clothes off. His jaw dropped when he saw my war-ridden body and he just kept staring at the Ranger and Seal tattoos.

Brooks said, "Bend the fuck over and spread your ass cheeks."

I said, "Come on now is this really necessary Pres? I'm not wearing a wire. You must've been talking with Ripper. He thinks I'm an undercover cop or fed. I'm clean, I swear."

The V.P Chang walked into view and ordered me, "Spread your ass cheeks so we can have a beer. Just get it over with, Prospect."

I grabbed my cheeks and passed their test. Then got dressed and asked, "Am I free to roll out now Pres?"

"Yeah, tell Hatchet to send a patched member or hang around next time. I don't like you very much. Now get the fuck out of here."

I rode back to the Brooklyn clubhouse fuming. Well, those two fuckers just got themselves ten years in prison. Both the Brooklyn and New Jersey chapters would be charged with interstate narcotics trafficking. I was going to enjoy locking that scumbag Brooks up. I arrived at the clubhouse around 6:00 PM due to traffic on the Garden State Parkway and 495. It sucks driving in traffic in a car but it's ten times worse on a bike.

Along the way I had stopped to call into Riddler to let him know that everything went down without a hitch and I was going to grab a bite to eat. Then I gave Kelly a call and spoke with her for twenty or so minutes. It was great to hear her lovely voice. It was odd I could've sworn I'd heard other people in the background when she picked up her cell phone. It sounded like she was shushing people. Maybe I was tired so I didn't say anything to her. I was just elated to hear her voice and get the rundown on what was happening with the kids and dogs.

I said, "Babe, you sound so sexy right now. What are you wearing?"

She said, "I was just working out. "I'm in my shorts and sports bra. I beat the shit out of the wooden man. It's not the same when you're not here Rick. I miss you so much and can't wait until this case is over and out of our lives. I gotta go, it's time to make dinner and walk the dogs. I'll kiss everyone for you. Rick, I love you forever."

I said, "Me too my love, always and forever. Be safe and keep your eyes open when you're outside shopping or hanging out. I'll call you this weekend sometime when I get a free moment."

We hung up and I downed my cheeseburger and fries and headed back to Brooklyn. Riddler and Hatchet greeted me as I got off my bike. I handed Hatchet two bricks of cash and went inside to grab a beer.

Hatchet said, "Nice work today, Prospect. I heard all about the bullshit Brooks put you through and I read him the riot act for doing so. He's up Ripper's ass and vying for a position with the Mother Chapter. Just ignore him and ride this shit out, You're close to the 180-day mark. The Roar at the Shore will be here in a few weeks. It's your first mandatory so be ready for it mentally and physically. The other chapters will put the prospects through the wringer to weed out the weak ones."

I said, "I'm not going down for anyone, Pres, This shit is my life forever."

That night I was running around fetching beers and food for the Excaliburs in the Cove. There were several muscle heads inside and staring us down. That was a huge mistake. One of them bumped into Mohawk and all hell broke loose. Fists were flying and boots were landing down hard on the guy's head that originally bumped into Mohawk. I was grabbed from behind by a six-foot gorilla and I sent the back of my head into the bridge of his nose. He fell to his knees and I sent a roundhouse kick into his temple and knocked him out. I dragged his ass out of the Cove then ran back inside to help my brothers.

Hatchet and Big Bear were squaring off with three guys. I ran over to them and joined in on the fight. I sent an elbow into the first guy's face that was across from Hatchet. He went down like a sack of potatoes. Then the second muscle head threw a hook punch at me. I caught his arm and slid my hands down to his right wrist, bent it inwards toward the inside of his forearm, and did a tight circular motion and he flipped to my right side.

I knelt against him, twisted his arm and it broke. Big Bear and Hatchet took care of the other guy. The fight finally broke up and the muscle heads ran to their cars and drove off. Mohawk shouted for us to come to the back.

The original guy was dead and bleeding from multiple stab wounds and deep hatchet wounds. They fucking killed the guy.

Hatchet said, "Get this mother fucker out of here. Mohawk, you, and Lizard get the fuck out of dodge until I tell you it's safe to come home. The heat is going to be all over us for this shit. Not to mention the Mother Club. Prospect clean this place up and lock it down for the night. Everyone take your colors off and hide them where no one knows where they are. Stay low until next Thursday. No club business is to be conducted until I say so. Everybody understand me?"

We all nodded and they threw the dead guy into the van and sped off. I started to clean up as fast as I could before the local cops came to the bar. I needed to report to the team about the events that had just taken place.

IX

Roar at the Shore

4th of July weekend had come as did the Roar to the Shore in New Jersey, which thrives in the wild woods because of the shore destination's centralized location on the East Coast. Located 150 miles or less from most major cities including Philadelphia, New York City, Baltimore, and Washington, D.C., there's no need to trailer your bikes to this rally. Hatchet explained to me that there would be several thousand bikers there. Many of them would be One Percenters but a lot would also be motorcycle enthusiasts who just enjoyed riding and partying. The club had stocked the van to the hilt with camping gear, barbecues, weapons, beer, plenty of booze, and drugs.

The club was told by Big Bear and Whippet to be on full alert in case of any retribution from the Marquis for the beat-down they took at Riverhead. The Mother Club was already there and had reserved a hotel for themselves and a few of the larger chapter officers. They had booked two entire floors and a party room for one of the Excaliburs who was coming home from doing a twenty-year stint in Elmira for the murder of a Highway Patrolman.

I had to bring both of my cell phones with me. One that I used when I was with the club and the other one was my NYBN cell phone. I didn't feel comfortable bringing the NYBN phone but Jimbo said.

"Rick, It's the only way I can keep the brass in the loop. You're not wearing a wire and they're breaking my balls about your photogenic memory. They think it's all bullshit and want to see us downtown after the weekend ends to dissect the operation. DC is up in arms saying we've got enough to bring in most of the Brooklyn chapter on the drug sales, weapon charges, and several of them on the murder charge."

I spoke in a low tone voice not to be heard, "Jimbo, listen to me, you tell those fucking pencil-pushing assholes that it's my ass on the line here and not to mention my family's lives. I'm going after the entire East Coast Excalibur Nation. With them or without them. I'm in too fucking deep and I can't afford to pull out. Tell them I'm not coming in until this operation is completed.

I'll go fucking dark if I need to. I can use the Guardians as a backup if you and the other teams want out too."

Jimbo sounded pissed off at me, "Hey, agent Batman, slow your roll and take a deep breath. Me and the team have your back. We're not leaving you out here to get burned in the frying pan. I've already spoken with Leo (Kahuna) from the Guardians and they're in this with you. I advised them it was the Excaliburs who were responsible for the murder of their member's niece. They want revenge and won't stop until justice and a pound of flesh have been taken.

They'll be at the Roar at the Shore also watching your six at all times. If anything jumps off they've got you. The Guardians are the only ones that can get close enough to where you are if something goes bad. They want these bastards more than we do. It's personal to them. They want blood and believe me. They're going to get it. With us or without us. Godspeed, Rick. Be careful and stay in touch as much as possible."

I said, "10-4, boss, talk to you later."

An hour later Guardrail gave the hand signal to roll out. It would be a 150-mile ride and I was looking forward to feeling the cool air on my face. The only thing bad about riding with the Excaliburs was it was extremely dangerous and those fucking fools rode like maniacs when they were on the open highways. They split lanes without signaling and cut cars off. It was like they were waiting for a motorist to say something so they could just beat the living shit out of them. That part I hated the most. Riding a Harley is serious business and it's extremely dangerous if a mishap happens.

We pulled over at a 76 gas station to gas up and get some drinks and junk food. Serpent and Steel came over to me and offered me a bump of coke. I declined and told them I had to report to my parole officer Tuesday morning. Serpent was telling me that he missed his brother who was on the run with Mohawk.

He said, "No, problem Prospect, more for us. Just be ready to party later." Serpent asked me, "Do you still want to buy that ounce of crank?"

I said, "Absolutely brother. I can unload that shit at the store. A lot of the weekend warriors love to party and have been asking me if I knew where to score any shit. I might see some of them at the Roar. I'll give you a heads-up if I do. If you want I can grab the shit now. I have some extra cash with me."

Serpent said, "Fucking ay bro, hang here for a minute while I get it from inside the van."

He handed me the ounce and I paid him $300.00. He said, "Why thank you sir, and please come back again."

All three of us laughed our asses off and mounted our bikes and waited for Guardrail's command to roll out. We arrived at the Shore at 4:00 PM and I found a spot that was secluded from the other clubs but was within earshot of the other Excaliburs. I wrapped a small piece of Ronin's hair onto the locks of my saddle bags. I was able to make it stick with some clear saddle soap. I did this to see if the hairs would be missing from the bags. I was certain that those nosey scumbags would be checking my bags out the entire weekend looking for wires and cash to steal. I wasn't a full patch yet and the bylaws didn't pertain to me while I was a prospect.

Hatchet told me to eat something quick and get to work. I'd be running around fetching beers and burgers for those fat fucks all weekend. Maybe even getting them drugs. The New Jersey, Boston, and Pennsylvania Chapters rolled in and set up their camps. The officers from the Boston, Jersey, and Pennsylvania chapters along with the Manhattan Chapter rode up to the hotel where the Mother Club was staying. An hour later I heard that old familiar jerkoff's voice. Ripper was yelling for me to haul my ass over to where his bike was parked.

Ripper said, "Prospect, my choke cable snapped and my rear tire is flat. Fix them and then clean my bike and make sure I can see my reflection in the gas tank. I want it looking like a fucking mirror"

I said, "Sure thing, Ripper. Let me just let my Pres know I'll be tied up for an hour or so."

"Don't Bother, "I'll tell Hatchet myself. Just fix my bike, Mr. Handyman."

Luckily for that maggot, Guardrail the road Captain had told me to bring some of my tools, a few kits of tire plugs, some CO'2 canisters to fill the tires up with air, and several Universal repair kits for emergency cable repairs. I plugged Ripper's tire quickly and then installed the emergency clutch cable. Part of me wanted to rig the cable so he'd crash but that would be a death sentence for me instantly. I cleaned his filthy bike and made it look brand new.

He kept his hog like he kept himself. Like a disgusting dirtbag. He had several other issues going on with his bike but I figured I'd let the road take care of that for me. The bike was a freaking death trap. He walked over to his hog and he was quite impressed and showed me his gratitude by punching me in the solar plexus.

He said, "Nice fucking work, Prospect. I hope you're ready to throw your fists later in the pit. I have a big surprise for you. Now go get me some food and a beer. Make it quick. I have a young chick that waiting to blow me."

I ran back and gave him his order and asked, "Will that be all, Sir?"

Ripper said, "Yeah wiseass that's it for now and don't call me sir again or I'll cut your fucking tongue out."

Hatchet called me over and I turned around smiling. I was thinking to myself, "Mother fucker by the time you tried to unsheathe your blade I'd have my Sog knife sunk so deep into your skull you'd be dead before you hit the fucking ground."

Hatchet said, Rick, "I've got some fucked up news for you. You're fighting tonight in the pit against the Mother Chapter's new Prospect. I know they don't normally have prospects but Ripper found this guy and he's an ex-MMA fighter. Dude fought in the UFC and was ranked number two for a short while. The guy is the real deal and there ain't no rules in the pit. If Arthur calls the fight it'll be a death match. Then you're going to have to kill this guy or be killed. I tried in vain to get this shit canceled but I lost the vote. Go rest or do what you need to do to prepare for this. I haven't seen their prospect yet. Go into the van and relax until I come and get you. I will have the other prospects cover for you. They're on their way out anyway. Might as well use them until they're gone for good."

The other members of the Brooklyn chapter were livid about what was going down later that night. It interrupted several of their plans and drug transactions with other chapters and bikers who were partying. 45 and Big Bear were fuming and went to the van to talk with me.

Big Bear knocked on the side of the van and said, "Prospect you okay?

I said, "Yeah I'm on the other side stretching."

45 said, "Rick man, we're sorry this is going down the way it is. Can we help with your training at all?"

Right then and there I could truly feel that most of the Brooklyn chapter had my back and were my brothers even though I wasn't a fully patched member yet.

I said, "No guys, I'm good, I just need to get my mind ready and my body will do the rest. Did you get a look at the guy I'm fighting?"

Big Bear who was as big as a house said, "Rick I gotta tell you, he's twice the size of me and moves quick as shit. I hope you're feeling fast and loose man. Hey man, drink a few of these and take a hit of this shit."

He handed me three Red-bulls and I declined the shot of crank he'd offered, I said, "I need my mind clear and focused. I can't have any drugs in me before I fight or see my parole officer. But thanks for the offer brother."

At 11:00 PM Ripper yelled to the chapters. "Excaliburs form a circle for the makeshift pit. Ripper said, "Frenchy will be collecting the bets for the Excaliburs and Doberman will collect the bets for the Centurions. Hatchet, go get your fighter. Ours is ready to pound him to a pulp."

Hatchet came over to me as I was kneeling and meditating. He said, "Rick, it's time. You've come too far to back out. Go kick that mother fuckers ass and we'll head back to the clubhouse right afterward. All the other guys have already packed their shit and are ready to roll out when this is finished."

I thought to myself, "Fuck, I better win this fight or one of them will want to ride my bike home and I can't let them discover the kill switch that Uncle Bobby installed. Also, if they bet money on me they'll be pissed that they lost their hard-earned cash selling dope.

I said, "Let's do this, Hatchet."

I walked through the members that formed the circle and saw my opponent. He was a monster of a man. 6'5, 270 Lbs. made of pure muscle. I figured him to be a grappler and that was fine with me. My Aki Jujitsu could hold up against the best of any fighter. I'd need to use my Kung Fu to win the fight.

Arthur said, "Ladies and gentlemen. I mean my criminally insane brothers of the Excalibur Nation. Tonight, we have a special event. Two of our prospects will fight each other either to the death or until one of them is maimed for life. Hatchet and Ripper present your fighters."

Ripper snarled, "This is the Manhattan Mauler."

Hatchet looked over to Whippet and 45. They mouthed my military nickname. Hatchet nodded in agreement and said, "This is The Rogue."

The crowd went wild and Ripper was furious and shouted, "Let's get it on King Arthur."

Arthur sent his right hand down and signaled us to begin the fight. The Mauler charged at me like a bull. He tried; the old wrestler Goldberg's move, the pile driver on me. I quickly sidestepped him and drove my right elbow down hard between his shoulder blades then kicked the back of his legs out from him. I mounted him and began to send elbows and fists into his face and jaw. The Mauler smiled and somehow was able to hip-toss me and reverse our positions. He was now on top of me.

He sent punches into my face that felt like sledgehammers. The second punch broke my nose then the third cracked my left orbital bone. I shook my head clear and kicked up and threw my right leg on top of his left shoulder and then wrapped my left leg around my right foot forming a triangle around his neck and squeezed his throat as tight as I could. He started to turn blue but then stood up with me wrapped around his neck and smashed me against the ground three times. My back exploded in pain and I could feel the shrapnel that hadn't been removed pierce through my skin. The ground began to soak with my blood.

Rage took over and my survival instinct kicked in. All my martial arts training and military training would need to come into play within seconds or I'd be a dead man. I kicked the Mauler off me and we stood toe to toe. He swung and I ducked, He tried to do a spinning back-kick, and I ducked. Then I spun him around and sent a crashing elbow into his nose and shattered it. I sent two shin kicks into his lower legs and broke his right and left legs, right below his kneecaps. Both breaks were compound fractures and the bones were sticking out from the skin. He screamed in pain and tried to hobble toward me. I sent a straight front kick into his chest and blood splattered out and he collapsed.

Arthur yelled, "Enough, Rogue is the winner. Go get these prospects medical treatment. The party is over."

Hatchet and Whippet grabbed me and carefully put me in the van. I said, "Get my pilers out of my saddlebag. Someone needs to pull the shrapnel out of my back and stitch me up. But make sure the shrapnel is away from my vertebrae. You'll cripple me if the metal cuts into my spinal cord."

Keg from The Centurions said, "I was a medic in the Army I will do it and then stitch him up. Just hold his ass down and give him a few shots of whiskey because this is going to hurt like hell. Pour at least half a bottle over the wound first. Get a few bottles over here pronto."

I said to Keg, "Go into the black bag in my right saddle bag. There's some stitching equipment and Demerol. Shoot me up with a CC. There's also lidocaine in there too, with some field dressing. I took a bunch of the kits with me when I retired from the Rangers."

After Keg pulled the shrapnel from my back I passed out for a few hours. When I woke up, Hatchet asked, "Can you ride, Prospect?"

I said, "Yeah, Let's get the fuck out of here."

X

Hit Night

I asked Hatchet if I could have a few days to recover and if it would be okay if I went and hung out with my ol' lady. He told me to take the week off and be back at the clubhouse for the weekend party. Then he said something I wasn't prepared for.

"Hey prospect, you did great last night. Did you see the paddle and baseball bat where the barrel has been cut in half hanging above the bar at the clubhouse?

I said, "Sure, I meant to ask you what they meant but didn't want to be nosey."

Hatchet said, "Well my friend, you're going to find out exactly what they're used for Saturday night. You get through this and you're in brother. But I ain't gonna lie, it's going to be painful and pure fucking hell for you this weekend."

"Mind telling me what I'm in for."

Hatchet explained, "Almost every member of the Excaliburs along the East Coast will be at the clubhouse this weekend to take one swing using the paddle or the bat onto your ass. I took a headcount of how many members will be attending the hit night. A total of 65 patches will be present. You and five other prospects will be going through the hit night together. Many patches will opt to just tap you on the ass. Others will swing for the fucking fences. So, be prepared for some pain. After that, we'll get the required signatures to patch you in. Will I be seeing you back here Saturday? If not, lay down your cut and there will be no hard feelings."

I said, "Fuck that, I'm in for life. Let the games begin. I'll see you Saturday, Hatchet."

I rode home in horrible pain. I just wanted to be in my wife's arms. I knew she'd be able to tend to my wound and call her unit to get a doctor over to properly fix my wound and get me the meds I needed to heal quickly. I told Jimbo I'd be off the grid for the next several days and would email him all the transactions I'd observed and engaged in. I let him know where to grab all the evidence of the drugs, I had purchased at the Roar. In a secluded area, I hid them in a hollowed-out tree in the south part of the park. I rode up to the house, parked the bike in front of the garage, and collapsed on the front lawn. Kelly and the dogs ran out and Kelly helped me into the house while the dogs stood guard on the front lawn until she let them inside.

I said, Babe, I need a doctor to come here ASAP. I'm not sure if that butcher nicked any of my organs when he took the metal out of my back. Whiskey please, I need a lot of whiskey, please babe, hurry."

Kelly said in a controlled voice, "How much more of this shit are you going to put yourself and us through. You're becoming one of them. Just by the way you're speaking with me. The violence that these bastards have you involved in is rubbing off on you. I need my husband back and the kids need their father back, Rick."

"I know babe, I'll be patched in this weekend. I just have to get through some kind of ritual called hit night."

She screamed, "What the fuck is hit night? It sounds like you're going to get your ass kicked. Is this investigation worth getting killed over? Damn it, Rick, I've done some crazy undercover work but this beats all of them hands down. I'm afraid I'm going to lose you. I'm starting to wonder if you've drifted over to the dark side. Have you gone dark on me, Rick Volpe? I want my husband back."

She started to cry and I sat up and hugged her tightly. I knew it was really bad and her temper had hit the roof when she had said the fuck word. I'd only heard her say that to me maybe a dozen times when we disagreed. The other times were when we were having sex. And she does say it a lot then.

I said, "Kelly, I haven't gone dark and we're almost at the end of the tunnel. Just stick with me on this okay I have several things in play and will tell you everything when the time comes. Just remember if something goes wrong you call Kahuna and the Guardians will be here within a half hour."

Kelly helped me off with my clothes and she took me into the shower and washed the dirt and scum from my body. Then she called a doctor to properly stitch my wound. He had told me that if he hadn't gotten to the house when he did the wound would have gone septic. He put me on a powerful antibiotic IV and gave me the proper pain meds to get me through the week. The doctor had also advised me that the shrapnel had narrowly missed severing my spinal cord.

Kelly took a call in the study and told me she had to run some errands and would be gone for several hours. She was actually heading out to work and working the case. Kelly had been looking on the dark web for illegal activity amongst OMGs. Then a whole page of things came up. A member of the Crypt Keepers, another support club of the Excaliburs who operated out of the Bronx, was selling two stolen 1992 Harley Davidson Softails for $2500 hundred each. She called Uncle Bobby and told him to tell me to buy them from the guy. She gave him a number to call and reminded Bobby that it came from a source of his, not her.

Bobby said, "No problem sweetheart. My lips are sealed. But I'm going to warn you. You're swimming in shark-infested waters not only going up against the Excaliburs but I don't want to be around when Rick finds out you've been working the case without his knowledge."

Kelly said with her Southern charm, "You're too sweet, Uncle Bobby, you really do love me. It's all good on my end. Thanks to you and Rick we're working with the Guardians and have things locked down here. Kahuna is getting ready to grab the Excalibur Riddler, on an arrest warrant. He skipped bail in 2020 and no one has caught up with him yet. The guy appears only when there's club business then goes back into hiding. He's a ghost. He's wanted on a rape and murder charge of a 21-year woman from Wantagh, NY. Kahuna has his location pinned down and will be snatching his ass up any day now. Can you tell Rick that this is going down?"

Uncle Bobby said, "Sure thing and I'll have Kahuna call Rick to let him know what's about to transpire within the next few days. He needs to be advised of this. It's going to bring war between the two clubs. It's inevitable. Take care and kiss the kids. When this is all over I'll hold a big barbecue in the parking lot of Hog City. Talk soon and for God's sake be careful out there."

Kelly blew him a kiss over the phone and then advised her team of what was going down. The Captain in turn reached out to Jimbo. Days later I was feeling better and getting my strength back. The wound had healed up nicely. Friday had come too quickly.

Kelly and I met up with the kids at a restaurant in Westchester and we had a great dinner together. I caught up on everything the kids were doing so far during the summer vacation. My UC phone was blowing up and Hatchet must've called me ten times. I answered the phone and put my finger to my lips to tell the kids to stay quiet.

"What's up, Pres?"

He said, "Prospect it's time. Get your ass down to the clubhouse and be ready. They moved the hit night to tonight."

"I'll be there in an hour; Pres just need to reseal my wound and shower up. I can't get this laceration infected. I'll be fucked if that happens. You know what I mean?"

Hatchet said, "Yeah, do what you need to do, but make it fast, prospect. All eyes are on you tonight."

Kelly said, "I know Hun, be careful. I'll bring the kids back to my mother's house. My sister will be taking them for the next few weeks."

I said, "Okay babe, I'm sorry to dump all of this on you. But I'm close to getting patched in. Then the investigation will be winding down. Kids, be good at your aunt's house and help her out when she needs a hand. I love you all and this will all be over soon."

The kids gave me big hugs and kisses and then I shared a long hug with Kelly and a passionate kiss and said, I love you to her. I jumped onto my bike and headed to Marine Park. I made it there in good time and was briefed by Whippet and 45 on what to expect.

45 said, "Prospect, I ain't gonna lie brother. This shit is the worse of your prospecting. It's going to hurt like a mother fucker. You probably won't be able to walk right for a week. Just suck it up and keep those ass cheeks tight as a clams ass."

Whippet chimed in, "Rick, you've more than likely been through worse with all that military training you did. So, just push yourself to the deepest limits that you can take. Don't worry about our chapter, we're not going to hit you hard. We'll just give your ass a tap with the paddle. It's the members' choice of how hard they want to swing on you. I can't answer for the other chapters, some dudes still think you might be an undercover or snitch. Either way man you're solid with us and we know you're not either. So, go get us some brewskis, and let's have a drink."

All the chapters had rolled in, five more prospects would be receiving the ass whipping as Big Bear put it. New Jersey, Boston, Pennsylvania, and the Mother Chapter from Manhattan were all there. A total of 75 patches were in attendance and ready to give it their one best swing for the fences.

The national President Arthur yelled out, "Let's get to hitting brothers. Prospects grab some chain link fence and prepare to get your asses hit into next week. Remember prospects whatever you do, don't stand up when a member is about to swing on you. Your back will never be the same. There aren't any lawsuits being filed against this club ever. If you even think of doing that. I'll fucking kill you myself and then let Ripper fuck your wives, then kill them. Do I make myself clear, fuck heads?"

We all said, "Yes. Mr. President."

All I kept thinking was how badly I wanted to break Arthur's neck, drag his dirtbag corpse into a ditch, and bury him.

Ripper yelled out, "Boston you're up first. Grab the paddle of the half bat and get to work. You only have one swing so, make that mother fucker count."

Borden the Boston Pres hit me first as I was number one in the line. He used the paddle and took a hard swing and I felt the wood come crashing against my ass cheeks. Scout the VP used the baseball bat on me and swung for the fences sending a bone-chilling pain through my body. I could feel my ass cheeks beginning to swell up. I knew it was going to be a long night. Bronson the Sergeant at Arms used the bat also and hit me so hard he lifted my feet off the ground.

The prospect from PA got up and said, "I'm out. I don't need this fucking insane bullshit. You fuckers are crazy."

Ripper walked over to him and laid him out with one sucker punch and dragged him into the Mother Chapters Van and handcuffed him to a long black pole that they'd installed for who knows what. The beating continued. After the members of the Boston Chapter had all gone. The PA Chapter was up next and they were out for revenge for losing the only prospect they'd sent through the club in two years.

Dayton the President used the paddle and hit me so hard I thought I was going to black out. Mayo the VP just tapped my ass cheeks with the paddle. He liked me and we had shared a few beers on the last run. One of the enforcers for the PA Chapter used the bat and swung on me lefty and his shot had lacerated my left ass cheek. Now Both ass cheeks were bleeding and I could feel the blood trickling down to the back of my legs.

Next up was New Jersey. And Brooks said to me, "This is for the last shipment, motherfucker. Next time you only speak when spoken to. I still think you're fucking Five-O."

He swung as hard as he could and hit my ass bone. I felt the pain riddle my body and dropped to a knee, got myself up again, and prepared to be hit by the Mother Club. Arthur went first and swung the bat hard against my ass and threw the bat to the VP, Lancelot. He surprisingly just tapped me. Ripper told the other members of the Mother Club to go before him. He would be the last to hit me. They got their whacks in and I felt like I was going to faint at any second. My chapter all just tapped me.

Hatchet said. "Give them a water break. It's been going on for an hour and a half. We need these last four guys to make it through to strengthen the club in case the Marquis make a move on us."

Hatchet handed me a cold bottle of water. He said, "You good bro? One more and you're done. I will put it to a vote that you get patched in by next week. I'll get all the required signatures. "

I said to them all, "Let's do this and start drinking."

That enraged Ripper and he said, "Bend the fuck over and grab that fence copper. Grab it higher so I can get a good shot in on you."

I grabbed the chain link fence higher and Ripper took a running start before he hit me and then I blacked out. Ripper had hit me low across my hamstrings. He didn't expect what had happened next. The bat had broken in half. He had no idea I trained my stomach, back, and legs to be hit with bamboo poles during my training with the Monks.

I woke up within a minute and asked, "Am I through, taking the beating?"

Arthur said, "Yeah go home and get some rest Prospect. You all did good tonight."

My ass cheeks were as swollen as basketballs and I could barely walk let alone ride my hog back to my UC pad. Jimbo and the team followed me but didn't dare try to come to the front door. I waved and let them know I'd be okay.

XI

The Deal

I rolled out of bed the Thursday after hit night had occurred. The swelling of my ass cheeks had finally gone considerably. I was able to sit normally and ride my bike. Going to work at the makeshift bike shop during that week was a nightmare. I needed to keep up my cover for the case. I knew they were still checking out my background. Whippet had strolled through the door of the store and said.

"Prospect Rick, How the fuck are you, brother? How's the ass healing? You know you really have to stop that gay shit with those hard-core biker men."

He let out a huge laugh and we were cracking up as I met him with the club's standard hug and hand shake.

"You crazy bastard Whip, what brings you here today?"

Then he hit me with a flurry of shit. Whippet said, "Prospect, I came here to speak with you about several things. Where can we talk in private?"

I said, "We can talk in the back of the store where the parts are. Just let me get the okay from my boss. I'll be right back. Grab some coffee and donuts while I go speak with him."

This was it. I'd possibly be able to get the VP on video and audio talking about engaging in illegal activities. I told the other undercover's to go outside in the front of the store after the equipment was ready to roll. Then I spoke into the undercover's earpiece that was posing as the owner.

"Uncle Bobby, it's me, be ready to assist the guys if they need any help if customers come inside the store. I'm in the middle of doing a possible deal with one of the club members."

Uncle Bobby said, "Already on it Rick. Be careful and watch what you say."

The three of us walked out front as Whippet was downing his fourth donut.

"Hey, VP, if you gonna give blow jobs out do it in the parking lot and wipe your mouth."

Whippet said angrily, "What the fuck did you say mother fucker?"

I pointed at his mouth and tossed him a napkin. He wiped the cream from the corner of his mouth and started laughing.

He said, "You little bastard."

I said to the undercover who was the boss. "We'll be in the back a few minutes boss. I'll skip lunch today okay? Thanks."

The undercover said, "No problem, Rick."

I pointed to the back and Whippet followed me there.

I asked, "What's up Whip?"

He was holding a vanilla envelope and handed it to me.

He said, "Sorry Rick, but you need to fill out your application all over. Ripper found a misspelled word and he told Hatchet to make you fill it out again. That's the first thing. Now comes some business I need to speak to you about. I have a guy on the inside at Fort Hamilton. He phoned me yesterday and let me know that two hundred pounds of C4 had fallen off a truck and wanted to know if I'd be interested in buying it. I told him I needed to speak with my guy. You're my guy. No one else knows how or what that shit is. We just know it blows shit up."

It will make some good fucking Christmas presents if we need to demo another club's clubhouse or house. We need this deal to go down brother and you're the only one that's got that type of knowledge in regards to military shit like this.

Third, we have the Laconia run in New Hampshire this Saturday, it's your second and final mandatory. You do all this shit for us and by the end of the weekend, you'll be patched in. Hatchet has secured all the signatures you'll need to be patched in. We do the deal tonight and leave for New Hampshire on Friday morning. The deal is set up at 11:00 PM at the Floridan diner parking lot. Myself, Big Bear, and 45 will be inside the diner in case any shit pops off.

You're picking up fifty pounds of C4 and some type of electrical devices that need to go with it."

I said, "Dude this is some heavy shit we're doing. What the fuck is the club planning on doing? Also, the electrical devices are called shunts."

Whippet said, "Prospect, what we're doing is called business. Are you in or not?"

Whippet then moved his vest to show me he was carrying a 38-snub-nose revolver.

I said in a pissed-off voice, "Hey Whip if you're trying to intimidate me by showing me that. I can tell you one thing; you better shoot all the bullets in that gun and kill me or you and I will be doing the death dance. I'm fucking in always. I just want to know what I'm getting myself into for the deal. It's called being prepared. And another thing. The electrical devices must be unassembled. I don't trust anyone but myself to assemble them to blow up the target. I've used plenty of them when I was in the Seals. I know exactly how to get them ready to trigger the blast and blow up anything or anyone that stands in our way."

Whippet handed me an envelope that contained twenty thousand dollars for the deal. I then asked him if I could buy a gun from him or one of the other members for the deal for my protection. It was against the rules for a prospect to carry a handgun but this was a different animal.

Whippet said, "Give me twenty minutes. You have 400 dollars on you. Jason has a brand new Interarm 45 automatic he's been trying to sell."

I said, "Yeah I can get an advance from my boss right now."

Whippet yelled out as he was leaving, "Prospect, start filling out that application again and have it completed by tonight before the deal goes down. The guy's name you're meeting is Kendrick he's a black Army dude. Jason will be here in twenty. I'm gonna have me some more donuts."

The agents and I couldn't believe the break we had just gotten in the case. But things also got much heavier with a military soldier selling explosives to the MC. After they left I'd needed to advise General Walton what was going down I'd take the lead on the transaction and he could deal with the soldier afterwards with the 101 unit from the MP's.

45 and Jason walked back into the store and we went into the back room. Jason handed me a brown paper bag that contained a box.

I asked Jason, "Can I check it out first to see if all the parts are functional?"

Jason said, "Sure have a look and let's get this done. I have a sweet little piece of ass waiting for me at the clubhouse. Ripper dropped her off for me in the morning. Fucking bastard charged me fifty bucks for her. Bitch can't be more than 16. You know what they say, bro if they bleed, they breed."

I was sickened by the statement but now I had him admitting that he was going to rape a 16-year-old girl. And I had Ripper on a human trafficking charge and without a doubt, a rape and kidnapping charge.

All I kept thinking was, "This club needs to be wiped off the face of the earth. The entire Excalibur nation needs to be eradicated."

As I was checking the 45 auto out, I noticed that Jason was also carrying an automatic in his waistband. Now I had both 45 and Jason on a Title 18 felony charge. Both of them were in possession of firearms, selling an illegal firearm to a federal agent and they were both convicted felons. Both of these scumbags were looking at 25 years minimum. The gun was perfect and I handed Jason the 400 dollars and they were on their way. But before they left, Jason grabbed five more donuts off the tray.

Jason was a real skell. Close to 270 pounds of fat and sleeved out with prison tattoos. The kind of guy a woman would never bring home to her parents. Jason was a beast and loved throwing any kind of drug into his system and the guy guzzled Jack Daniels like it was water. One thing was for sure he knew how to handle a throwing axe.

45 said, "See you in a few hours in Brooklyn. Bring the application and the money. Talk to you later, Prospect."

Jimbo and the team met me at the Odd Lot at around 8:30. He handed me the application that I'd sent over to him earlier and it was completed. Those fuckers really made it hard to get through the process. I had to have all my mail made out to my undercover name and that included the junk mail, where and who I worked for the past twenty years. They'd even gone as far as to go to my old high school and asked Mr. Demott to see the yearbook for the year I graduated from. Ripper was infuriated when he saw my picture with my undercover name under the photo. Demott had really come through for me.

They spoke with my old neighbors who of course were undercovers also. They were leaving no stones unturned. The PI actually had the balls to call my general on two more separate occasions to try and cross him up.

General Walton was too sharp for the guy and on the second call he said, "This will be the last time you call me about Lieutenant Mason. Am I making myself clear, sir?"

Jimbo said, "Listen, Rick, this is some heavy-duty shit you're about to pull off. I haven't even called this into the SAC or the AUSA yet. If this deal goes sideways we're all fucking toast and will be flipping burgers at McDonalds. I pray this grunt doesn't include the devices to blow this shit up. Godspeed brother and be extra careful."

Then Jimbo said, Hold up there cowboy. What the fuck are you carrying in your waistband. That firearm hasn't even been processed yet with our firearm techs. You know they have to make it street-safe before you get it back. We need to log that cannon into the system as part of a gun transaction. We also need photos of the gun."

"Jimbo, I can't go to the meet without the gun I just brought it. It'll raise suspicion. Let's just get this deal done and I'll log it in later tonight with the techs. If you want take some photos with your phone."

Jimbo said, "You really are a fucking Rogue, Rick. You've got the team going half batty and some of them want a vacation from you."

"Hey, they want out, fine. I'll do this shit on my own. I don't need guys on the team that are bitching and crying about time off or that I'm too fucking wild in the street. If they think they can do better I'll gladly switch with them. I'm outta here. See you later."

Agents Peck, Poole, and Reynolds asked Jimbo to be let out from the operation upon completion of the deal. It was getting too hairy for them and they wanted to go back to being pencil-pushing douchebags. That was fine with me. Less is best as far as I was concerned.

I arrived at the Florian diner at 10:50 and hit the kill switch on my bike. I went into my saddle bag and retrieved the gun and cash. For this deal, I had my Zippo lighter on and fully charged. The wire was already running and recording everything to the team. I could see Jason and 45 in the club's van in the corner of the lot and out of site.

I walked into the diner to grab a cup of coffee. To my surprise, the Army soldier was sitting at a booth eating a ham and cheese sandwich. He looked up and saw me and nodded, then he held his hand up and mouthed, "Give me five minutes."

I nodded and took my coffee out to the parking lot. The soldier came out and introduced himself to me.

"Hey friend, I'm Kendrick, and who may I ask are you? Where's Jason and 45 at?"

I said, "I'm Rick Mason. Jason and 45 couldn't come tonight. They told me you have something we'd be interested in?"

Kendrick said, "Follow me to the black Honda over there in the rear of the parking lot. I hope you don't think you're riding out of here with 50lb's of C4 on your bike. The minute you start that fucker up its blow the entire town of Mill Basin to kingdom come."

"No, I have a ride coming here to transport the shit back to the clubhouse."

With that, Kendrick opened the trunk of his car. He pulled a green Army blanket from the top of a crate to show me the 50 pounds of C4 and the devices to make the C4 explode.

Kendrick said, "You got the money?"

I handed him the twenty thousand in the brown envelope and he took his sweet ass time counting it. Then he said.

"Hey man, you're two grand short. I said $22,000,00, not twenty grand. I even threw in the devices."

I said, "Listen soldier boy. The deal was for twenty K so let's get this over with and we both can be on our way. Fair enough? And if this goes as planned I'll deal with you myself and buy an additional fifty pounds of C4 from you in a few weeks. But let's get this deal wrapped up and then we can cut the middleman out and deal with each other. Here's my cell phone number. Also, I have a question. Are the devices unassembled or ready to go? "

Kendrick said in an excited voice, "Fifty pounds will run you fifty thousand with the electric devices. The devices are not ready to go. You have to assemble them yourself. Here are the directions on how to connect the wires and where to place the device into the C4. We, good with all this shit, Rick"

I said, " Fucking ay, we're all good and you got a deal, Kendrick."

He took the crate out and I hid it behind a bush and waited for him to drive off. We had agreed to do another deal in the coming weeks at the same place. Five minutes later Jason and 45 rolled up and grabbed the crate and put it in the back of the van.

Jason dropped the crate down hard. I stood in disbelief and waited for my life to end in a fierce explosion. Luckily, the dropping of the crate didn't set off anything off.

I said in a low voice ."Take it easy with that shit bro, it's got the devices inside the crate along the side of the C4. You want to blow us all up?"

45 slapped Jason in the back of the head and said to me, "Take the rest of the night off, Prospect. You did good tonight. Hatchet texted me and said for you to be ready for the Laconia run this weekend. We're riding out with the New Jersey Chapter to New Hampshire. The light is at the end of the tunnel prospect. Get you're riding and camping gear ready tonight and be at the clubhouse by 9:00 AM tomorrow."

XII

The Laconia Run

I phoned Jimbo and let him know there would be no early vacations. We were heading out to New Hampshire in the morning for the Laconia run. I reminded him to get a motel that was at least twenty miles from the camping site. 45 also told me that the Jersey chapter and The Centurions would be riding with us. The pack of riders would be close to 100-strong.

That meant it would be even more dangerous for myself and any other patches and prospects riding. I went back to my UC pad and got prepared. First I trained for an hour then showered and got all my gear together. I woke up at 7:00 AM and put the necessary equipment in my saddle bags. The patch kits and the emergency cables along with my tools. I took the chance and brought the Zippo lighter. I stuffed my firearm deep into the right side saddle bag in case I needed it. I had concluded that the operation was now a rogue operation. All the rules were out the fucking window. I'd suffer the consequences with the brass later when these scumbags were all behind bars.

This run would have me under the microscope for sure. Ripper would be doing his best to prove to the club that I was an undercover cop. I'd do my best to prove I wasn't. It was a live-or-die time for me. I rode into the lot of the clubhouse and was greeted by Hatchet, Whippet, Big Bear, and a few other club members. Twenty minutes later Doberman, Keg, and XXX from the Centurions rode in. Several more arrived a few minutes later two new greasy unkempt scumbags who were prospecting for the Centurions. I'd purchased some crank and coke from them when they were hang arounds.

I'd purchased crank and cocaine from both of them when they were hang arounds.

The Jersey chapter rolled in around 10:30 and Guardrail went over the routes we'd be riding on. The Centurions would be riding behind the Jersey chapter patches. The officers would be upfront and would be riding in sequence with their respective ranking officers.

Guardrail gave the command to roll out and 100 hundred bikers took to the road. Four hours later we gassed up on RT-1 to top off our tanks.

Guardrail said, "We've got about an hour left in the ride so stay in a tight formation. As you can see we're not getting much love from the motorists and one wrong move from anyone will be a disaster. No funny business out there. Let's ride, brothers."

About twenty-five minutes into the final part of the ride, Serpent decided to pull ahead of Steel and Blade. He hit a pothole in the road, and lost control of his bike, and almost wiped out Jason and me. I swerved to the left and then the right to avoid Jason.

Then it happened Serpent hit a motorist who had slowed down in the left lane to avoid hitting any of the bikers in the formation. Serpent turned slightly to the left and went across the divider right into an eighteen-wheeler head first. Guardrail and Hatchet suddenly stopped their bikes and the formation came to a screeching halt. Serpent was DOA and several of his body parts were scattered along the highway. His bike was totaled and the trucker was a total wreck.

The trucker swore to Hatchet and Doberman, "He came out of nowhere. He just flew right into the front of my truck. I couldn't react quickly enough. Oh my God. I'm so sorry for what happened. Please believe me. I had nowhere to maneuver the truck. There were cars and trucks on both sides of me."

Hatchet said, "We know man. Just call an ambulance and the cops to get here ASAP."

The trucker ran back to his truck and called 911. But the first responders were already heading to the crash. People that were in their cars had already called it in. I phoned Jimbo while the others were looking around in a state of shock.

I said, "Jimbo, we've got an issue here on RT-1. Serpent is dead. He tried to pass another member in front of him in the formation, lost control of his bike, and went right into an eighteen-wheeler going in the opposite direction. He's DOA. I won't be able to call you for a little while so, stay put and have the Guardians ready to back me up if shit hits the fan. Tell Kahuna I'll meet him Saturday at the South West part of the lake. I gotta go now."

"Hatchet said, "We wait for all the authorities to leave, then we roll out. I need to call his mother and father to let them know what has happened. They live here in New Hampshire. Prospect, looks like you and I will be taking a ride to their house later to offer our condolences."

The authorities finished up around 3:00 PM and we were back on the road. Everyone's mood was somber. There was no high-fiving or drinking. A few guys and their ol' ladies snorted some cocaine and crank. To be honest I couldn't blame them seeing that wreckage and their buddy Serpent killed. We pulled into the campsite and the other clubs that were there had heard about what had happened. I saw Ripper and he headed right over to me.

Ripper said. "Prospect I was going to break your balls this weekend and try and force you to quit or admit you're a rat or a copper. But seeing that your chapter just took a huge loss. I'm giving you a freebie this weekend. Don't fucking get used to me being nice to you. I don't like you one bit and if I get the chance to stomp you. I will in a heartbeat. Now get the fuck out of my face."

I put two of Ronin's dog hairs on the locks of my saddle bags. I knew that someone was going to go through my bags this time. Hatchet and 45 came over to me.

Hatchet said, "Don't think he doesn't want to try and beat your ass. He was warned by the big dog to lay off. We're doing the preparations for Serpent's funeral to be held here at the site. He'll be cremated tomorrow. I just spoke with his mother and she told me not to ever show mine or any of our faces near the funeral home or their house. So, we'll be giving Serpent a full OMG funeral and our support clubs will be in attendance. You and the other prospects will be running around like dogs for the rest of the weekend."

I said, "What do you need me to do now, Pres?"

Hatchet said, "Go get me and 45 a six-pack of beers, a few burgers, and a rack of ribs. Get yourself something to eat too."

Saturday night came and all the members and the Mother club formed a circle around Serpent's cut and what was left of his belongings. His body parts were delivered to the morgue where his family would have a closed casket wake and funeral.

Arthur spoke first, "We're all gathered here tonight to pay our deepest respect for our fallen brother Serpent. He died doing what he loved best. Riding with his Excalibur brothers. His name will go on the wall along with our other fallen brothers. So, let us pay tribute to this Excalibur warrior and send his soul into the lake. Give me a hell yeah for Serpent."

We all yelled out in unison, "Hell Yeah, Serpent, Hell Yeah, Serpent."

Arthur and the entire Mother Club approached me after the funeral and said, "Prospect, walk with us."

Arthur waved for the officers of the Brooklyn Chapter to come over and join him.

Arthur said, "Hatchet here says you did really good for us the other night and I wanted to personally thank you. I know that wasn't your typical bullshit deal. He also advised me that you know your way around planting the C4 and detonating it. I read your jacket. You're quite the war hero. Aren't you?"

I just nodded and said, "I guess you can say that. Nothing that special about me. I'm just a guy trying to fit into the world and the Excalibur Nation, sir."

Arthur then said "We're going to blow the shit out of several enemy clubhouses soon and I want you to lead the mission for us. Are you good with that, Prospect?"

I said, "Yes sir, Arthur. I'll do as commanded for the Excalibur Nation."

He looked at Hatchet and said, "Patch this badass in tomorrow night before we leave the Lake. I want all the chapters here when you do it."

Arthur looked straight at Ripper and asked him, "Ripper, you good with that? Maybe after he gets patched in, you and the Prospect can give it a go in the pit if you're still game. But not until the mission is completed. Now let's go celebrate the life of our fallen brother, Serpent."

The rest of the night was going smoothly until I saw Ripper's arm around a young woman who looked to be around 16 or 17 years old. I got up closer to have a look, but Ripper twirled her around as I approached the area he was in. I got a good look at her face and committed it to memory. As they were walking away she held her hand behind her, tucked her thumb inside her hand, extended the four fingers straight then closed her fist around her thumb. She did the gesture three times.

I slipped away and contacted Jimbo. I said, "We have a situation. A teenage girl was with that scumbag, Ripper and he had his arm around her in a forceful manner. As they were leaving she did the abducted sign behind her back. Send one of the backup team in and have him say he's the girl's uncle and they've been looking all over for her. Then have him just grab her and leave the Lake area as fast as he can. Contact the Guardians for backup. I can't get involved, I'm surrounded by eighty Excaliburs and I'm about to be patched in tomorrow night."

Jimbo said, "10-4 I'm on it as we speak. I sent Kahuna a text. We've got it handled from here. What is Ripper's location?"

I said, "They're in cabin number ten hanging out just partying. I heard Ripper call her Callie. You can do a snatch-and-grab or go the drama route and have the agent act like the girl's uncle. If things get bad, tell him to snap a picture of Ripper and the entire group and have the Guardian swarm in. They're allowed to be armed because they're Fugitive Recovery Agents and Body Guards. I gotta get back now."

Ten minutes later agent Brock Watkins walked into the area and spotted Ripper and the girl sitting on a log outside the cabin. He was groping the girl and she was clearly upset about it. Tears were running down the cheeks of her face.

Watkins walked up to them and said, "Callie, is that you? Dear God, your mother and father are worried sick and the entire family has been searching all over New York, New Jersey, and New Hampshire. Come hug your Uncle Brock and let me thank this nice gentleman for taking care of you."

Ripper smartly let the girl go and she ran over to Agent Watkins. Ripper asked, "What did you say her name was?

Watkins said, "Callie, why do you ask? I figured you already knew her name. Is there more to this that I need to know? Shall I contact the authorities?"

Ripper said, "Take the little bitch the fuck out of here, don't let me see you or her around this lake again."

Watkins said, "Thank you, for locating her for our family. We're so appreciative of you. What did you say your name was? There's a ten thousand dollar reward for the person that found her. We'll mail you a bank check as soon as I get home. What's your mailing address, sir?"

Ripper actually gave his real name to Agent Watkins. And told him that he was Louis Bowen and he lived at 3270 Broadway Ave, apartment 12 G, NY, NY. Agent Watkins thanked him again, walked the girl to his car, and sped off.

She was safe and in NYBN custody and would be home by the end of the night. I'd stopped that bastard from committing sodomy and rape on the underage girl and possibly saved her life.

XIII

Patched In

Sunday afternoon came and Hatchet yelled to Whippet. "Hey, where the fuck is Riddler. He knows this is a mandatory run. Get that fucker on the phone and tell him I want his ass here before 6:00 PM tonight. I don't care who's after him. Tell him to wear a fucking wig and dress if he has to. Just get here for the prospects' induction into the club. If he's a no-show then I'll have him put out bad and he knows what will happen to him next."

Whippet said, "I'm on it Pres. No worries. If I have to go and pick his ass up myself then so be it."

I was listening to the whole conversation between the President and VP. I made my way a little closer to Whippet when he made the call.

Whippet spoke in a low voice, "Hey Rid, buddy, you need to ride out to Laconia right now. Hatchet is on a fucking warpath and he's fuming that you're not present for this run. Get your ass into gear and get here before 6:00 PM tonight. We're patching, Rick in. Hatchet told me that if you're not here before 6:00 PM you'll be out bad."

(Out Bad means you've been excommunicated from the club and you're on bad status in the motorcycle club. No one can talk to you or acknowledge you. The Excaliburs take all the member's possessions. His bike, colors, and anything else that has the Excalibur name attached to it).

Riddler said, "Fuck me, I'll head out now. He knows the Feds, the locals, and every damn bounty hunter are looking for my ass. I get caught Whip and I'm going away for life. I already have two prior felonies against me. This will be the third strike rule, the Feds will argue for a life sentence, and I won't be eligible for parole. I'll be there in a few hours and then I'm going to ask to be released from the club. It's time for me to retire from this OMG shit. I'm getting too old and tired from all of the partying and riding. See you in a few, brother."

I'd heard the entire conversation and texted Jimbo with the intelligence I'd just gathered. "I wrote, Jimbo, have Kahuna and The Guardians grab Riddler when we roll out in the morning. He told Whippet he'd be traveling on I-95 instead of

Route 1. Kahuna can grab his ass there. Good luck. Keep that scumbag away from any phones and do not, I repeat do not, try and flip his ass. If you do that, my cover will be blown. Jimbo, we have 90% of them on the RICO Act. That includes all of the East Coast Chapters and the Mother Club. And don't forget about The Centurions and The Crypt Keepers. I'm going to tear this whole fucking thing down. One perp at a time. I'm working on seeing if they'll sell me some C4 directly. That will be the final nail in the coffin."

Riddler pulled into the camping site at 5:30 PM and Hatchet headed right over to him. They exchanged a brotherly handshake and hug.

Hatchet yelled over to me, "Prospect, grab us four beers and a few burgers. This man is parched and hungry as hell."

I said, "Yes, Pres, I'm on it."

I grabbed the beers and ran them over to Hatchet and said hello to Riddler. Then I raced over to the barbecue, rounded up six burgers, and put all the fixings on each of them. I had three plates full of food. I felt like a damn waiter in a diner. The two of them pounded the beers down along with their food. I went to take a leak and check on my bike to make sure it was in one piece and that no one had rifled through my saddlebags.

Sure, enough the right saddlebag lock had been left open and Ronin's dog hair had dropped to the ground. I heard footsteps coming up from behind me. They were very heavy footsteps. I stood up slowly and turned around. Ripper was standing six inches away from me.

He said, "I told you mother fucker, that I'd catch you dirty. Now I have your ass and you'll be out of here. But not before I break some of your bones first."

I said, "Well, Ripper, if you want a shot at the title then let's just fucking dance right now. I'm sick of your bullshit."

Ripper then pulled out the 45 automatic that I'd purchased from Jason.

Ripper said, "Prospect, you know the rules. No prospect can carry a firearm while they're prospecting. You broke the rules. Now you're out."

I said, "You fucking scum-sucking pig. You broke into my saddlebags. You broke a rule too. No stealing from a club member. I want to speak with Hatchet and Arthur."

Ripper said, "They're on their way now, Ricky Boy."

Ripper told Arthur that I was in possession of a firearm. And was insubordinate to him. He screamed in Arthur's face saying,

"I want his head on a stake. I want this copper in the pit. I'm going to tear his eyes out and skull fuck him to death."

Hatchet said, "Ripper, I gave him permission to buy the gun for the deal he made for us. That deal was the largest and most dangerous thing this club has ever been involved in. I didn't see your ass volunteering to make the C4 purchase. So, lay the fuck off the guy, and let's patch him in. You want his ass in the pit then wait until he's a full patched member to fight it out with him."

Arthur said, "I agree with Hatchet. Patch Rick Mason into the club. And Ripper not another fucking word out of your mouth tonight. You already almost got us busted with the underage girl you took to the lake. You're getting stupider by the minute."

Hatchet threw me a brown paper bag and a black rolled-up shirt.

He said, "One last thing Prospect. Recite the Bylaws to us."

I said nervously, 1) Never steal from another member. 2) Never lie to another member. 3) Never mess around with an ol' Lady or a woman that's a member's property. 4) Never cause another member to get arrested. 5) Pay your dues on time to your chapter. 6) Never miss a mandatory run.

Hatchet said, "Perfecto, open the bag brother."

It had my top rocker that said Excaliburs and the middle patch of a skull with wings and two crossed swords under the skull head. Then a diamond 1% patch and my club name in a small rectangle patch. It said, Rogue.

Arthur said, "Everyone hold up your cups and meet your new brother, Rogue. 45, grab a paddle and distribute ten hits to Ripper for stealing from another brother."

Ripper was fuming and grabbed a bench and took the shots from 45 who laced into him as hard as he could. I knew from then on, Ripper would be out for blood and I was fine with that. It was going to be his blood, not mine.

All the members came over to me and congratulated me. All except, Ripper. Now I had that fucker Ripper for kidnapping and I was sure rape, sodomy, and murder. The other members of the mother club would also be charged with a federal crime of asportation of a kidnapped victim. I needed to get one of the club members to roll on Ripper for any other kidnappings. I knew that wasn't his first rodeo in committing the heinous act. Little did I know that was going to be very soon. I sewed the patches on perfectly and put my Excalibur shirt on so Kahuna, Jimbo, and the team could see that I was a fully patched member of the Excaliburs. I partied hard the rest of the night and we rolled out around 6:00 AM the next morning.

In the early morning, I snuck out to meet up with the Guardians and Kahuna.

I said, "We have to make this fast, Kahuna. I can't get busted being seen here with you. Not yet. We'll take these fuckers down together. Riddler is taking the I-91 to the 95 to get back to New York. Snatch his ass up and bring him to Jimbo where he'll be placed into our custody. The bail bondsman is with Jimbo and my team. They're waiting for you with your check upon delivery of the fugitive. Good luck brother. This thing is winding down so be careful out there. I have to head back."

Kahuna said, "Holy shit, you were patched in last night weren't you?"

"Yes sir. I'm the very first undercover to ever infiltrate these bastards. I'm quite sure we can nail ninety percent of them on the RICO Act and narcotic charges. Many of them are going away for murder and kidnapping too. And your member will get justice for his niece. That I promise you."

Kahuna said, "We'll just let me know what you need me to do and I'm there along with the Guardians to assist you and the NYBN. Great job, Rogue. Be safe."

I snuck back into camp and twenty minutes later Hatchet yelled, "Time to wake up boys and girls. We ride out after breakfast. So, pack up and make sure you have all your gear. Rogue double-check that you've got your tools and parts for any breakdowns. We have parted ways with Riddler who took Route I-91. Two hours later we stopped at a gas station that had a convenience store and a bathroom. I hit the head and checked my UC phone messages.

There was one from Kahuna, "Brother we grabbed Riddler on I-91 right before it he went to exit onto I-95. I'm with Jimbo and your team. Be careful you're out there alone. I'm sending some of the Guardians to ghost you in case anything jumps off. They'll be several miles away but have your back. Be safe, great job today."

I wrote back quickly, "10-4 and congrats. Remind Jimbo, no trying to flip Riddler and keep that scumbag away from the phone. He's not to get his one phone call until this investigation is completed. Tell Jimbo to take him to one of our black sites. I don't even want to know which one he's bringing him to."

I erased all the messages and stashed the undercover phone into a hidden pocket that I'd sewn inside my leather vest. The thickness and padding of the vest made it easy to hide wires and my phone if I needed to have them on my person. Most times I didn't. Only in emergencies.

We hopped onto our bikes and Guardrail put up the signal to ride. We arrived back at the clubhouse at 5:00 PM, ordered some pizza, and spoke about the events that had transpired during the run and the club once again toasted me as their new fully patched brother. We had a moment of silence for our fallen brother Serpent.

45 hung Serpent's small axe on the wall next to the other brothers who had died or were in jail. I began to realize that even though the Excaliburs were ruthless criminals they did have a deep sense of loyalty and honor. They truly were a tight-knit family. In a weird sense of way. I felt like many of them were my brothers-in-arms. More so, than my law enforcement brothers. I had the brass always trying to put an end to the investigation and team one had pulled out of the investigation altogether. I'd make sure to meet up with those turncoat cowards one day. I knew they'd all put in for transfers so as not to be harassed by the real agents who were doing deep-cover operations.

XIV

Riddler

Kahuna and the Guardians placed Riddler into the custody of the NYBN. The bail bondsman handed Kahuna $75,000.00 in cash. Jimbo told the Guardians that he'd be needing their assistance in the near future and to be on standby. He also advised them that they would be well compensated for their efforts in helping the NYBN during the investigation. There was a U.S. Marshal and Judge in the office and all the Guardians were sworn in as deputies of the Marshal Service and were given federal powers to make arrests when the time came to take down the East Coast chapters of the Excaliburs, the Centurions, and the Crypt Keepers.

Agent Howell sat across the desk from Riddler and said, "Daniel Hoffman AKA Riddler. Are you a big Batman fan? Is that why your nickname is the Riddler? Let's get down to business, shall we? You skipped bail from your rape and murder charge and your bondsman is pretty pissed off at you. It looks like we'll be adding kidnapping charges to the rape and murder of the Manorville teenage girl. What makes a monster like you commit such vile acts against young women? You're facing forty years or more for those crimes. And in addition to all those charges, we have you on firearm possession, narcotics trafficking, and selling narcotics to an undercover officer while being a convicted felon."

Jimbo screamed into the intercom. "Stop the interview, now, Agent Howell."

Howell came out from inside the room and asked, "What the hell, boss? I was just getting to the good stuff. I could see it in his eyes. He's ready to roll on his crew."

Jimbo said, "What the fuck are you doing? We have an agent that's knee-deep inside their organization and you tell him he sold to an undercover cop. By now he's already figured it's Rick. You're done, you're off this investigation. Go see the ASAC and put in for a transfer immediately. I don't ever want to see your fucking face in this office ever again. And another thing. If Rick Volpe gets one scratch on him. I'm holding you accountable. I promise you I'll have your shield. Now get the fuck out of my face."

Jimbo entered the interrogation room and sat across from Riddler. "Hello, Daniel. I'm Agent James McClure. I'm the head field agent for this office. Do you want a drink or a sandwich? If it makes it easier for you, just call me Jimbo."

Riddler said, "The guy that was in here before said I'm facing 40 years to life. Was he bullshitting me or what?"

Jimbo said, "Well, Daniel, he was telling you the truth. All except the nonsense about selling to an undercover cop. That was just to scare the living shit out of you. I know all about you Excalibur guys, you don't get scared easily. You're badass mother fuckers right. Well, hear me now my friend. You're going down for federal capital murder, rape, and kidnapping. You're a two-time felon and this is strike three for you. That's life baby. I'm going to make sure you're cellmate is the biggest craziest black inmate inside whatever prison you go to. I'll make sure that the prison guards let him know you're a racist piece of shit, white supremacist."

Riddler's hands shook and he started bouncing both of his knees like he had to take the biggest piss of his life.

Riddler said, "What if I give you a serial rapist and killer all in one package? Will that help knock some time off my sentence and keep me away from the Negros and Latino's? I can't be housed with them; I need to be with my brothers or the Aryan nation."

Jimbo said, "First you're signing a complete confession to the rape, kidnapping, and murder of the Wantagh woman, Ashley Wheeler. Then I'll call the AUSA and see if he's willing to cut you a deal. I'm telling you this one time only. You fucking bullshit me on any of the information you provide. I'll string you up by your balls and gut you like a pig. By the way, you don't get a phone call until I say you do. We're moving you to a secure location where you're safe from your so-called brothers."

I got a 911 text from Jimbo and it said, "Call me ASAP we've got 411 coming in from Riddler."

I was home at my UC pad and called him right away. "Jimbo, what the fuck are you doing to me? You're going to get me killed. I don't give a shit about the information that guy is offering. Fucking throw his ass into a black site until this investigation is over. I'm going home to be with Kelly for the next two days. Don't call me while I'm with my wife. This is a total nightmare and I'm not going to get out of this alive. Reach out to Kahuna and tell him to be at my house later tonight with his president. Talk to you later."

Jimbo called the AUSA and then took Riddler to an undisclosed motel in the Bronx. An hour later the AUSA Bryce Cobb walked into the room with a stenographer.

Bryce introduced himself and said, "So, Mr. Hoffman, let's hear about this serial killer."

Riddler was just signing his name to his confession and handed the paperwork to Jimbo, who in turn gave it to Bryce.

Riddler said, "The man I'm about to tell you about is the most deadly and sadistic Excalibur that the club has. He goes by the club name, Ripper. His real name is Lance Jefferson but he changed it to Louis Bowden. He hated that his father was black and his mother was white. He's really into the white supremacist shit too and is tatted with all of those Nazi signs and crosses. Ripper is one bad mother fucker and will kill anyone that tries to take him down."

Bryce said, "We know all about Ripper. Now stop wasting my time and give me details of these supposed rapes and killings. Otherwise, you're going straight to Otisville."

"Riddler spoke nervously and said, "Okay, Ripper, told me one night while we were drinking at the Roar at the Shore back in 2019. He said he has four dead women buried in the cement of the boiler room in his building. The maintenance guy who works there is a meth head and Ripper gives him drugs to get access to the room."

Jimbo asked, "How and where did he get the women he killed?"

Riddler said, "That's the easy part. He takes the Mother Club's black van to Grand Central Station or Penn Station and looks for young girls who are wandering around aimlessly. Then he buys them some food and offers them a ride back home or to his place to crash out. Then he brings them to a place he calls his dungeon and he has sex with them and beats the living shit out of them. If he thinks the club will want a piece of that chicken ass he won't bruise them up too much. Then he takes them to Arthur who bangs them out and then the girls are passed around the club. Then they get sold to one of the other chapters. The only thing is four of the chicks Ripper beat so badly he killed them after he'd raped them. He turned them inside out if you know what I mean. He buried them in the concrete of the boiler room. I think, there's more than four chicks down there."

Bryce asked, "What about the other girls that lived? Where are they now?"

Riddler smiled, "Man, they're club property. They became Mama's or club meat. They're so fucking strung out on crank they can't even remember their own names."

Jimbo asked in an angry voice, "Did you ever buy any of the girls from Ripper, Daniel?"

"Fuck yeah, She only cost me a hundred bucks. I named her Violet and she's my property now. She's my ol'lady. And it wasn't Ripper that sold her to me. It was the fucking King himself, Arthur." Riddler said smiling.

Jimbo stood up and said, "You stupid bastard, you aided and abetted a violent felon in a kidnapping and rape charge. Are you holding the girl against her will? And I want to know her real name so I can get her back to her parents."

Riddler said, "I don't know her real name. She's just Violet to me and I love her."

Bryce asked, "How old is Violet?"

"She's of age. She's eighteen years old and can make her own decision if she wants to stay or go home. Now do I get my deal or what?"

Bryce said, "You get your deal when the bodies are recovered. If you've lied about anything today, I'll make sure you never see the light of day again. Agent McCure bring Mr. Hoffman to the Metropolitan Correctional facility and have him placed in PC." (protective custody).

Jimbo texted me and gave me all the grisly details of that maniac Ripper. I told him I'd call Kelly to help him locate the bodies in the boiler room at 3270 Broadway. She could use the dogs.

I called Kelly, "Hun it's me. I need you to do me a big favor. Get the dogs over to the Manhattan office and meet Jimbo there. He may have bodies that need to be located at a building. Use Ronin and Talia and watch out for boobytraps in the boiler room. The US Marshal is there to swear you in and deputize you to assist in the search and recovery operation.

They'll deputize the dogs as well in case anything happens to one of them or they attack someone. Also, I want to tell you how much I appreciate the work you've done on the case with your unit so far.

You didn't need to go behind my back and get sworn in. I'll always back your play in life babe. You're the reason my heart beats and I draw breath to breathe every day. I wish I was home with you and in your arms right now. I was coming home tonight but with the new intel we received today on the arrest of Riddler. I'm stuck here with these crazy bastards. You know I was patched in right?"

She said, "Jeez, how the hell did you know? Did Uncle Bobby or Jimbo tell you?"

I said, "No I could tell by your movements and the way you were trying to be your natural self. I saw your lip and nose doing those little twitches when you're nervous or horny."

"Oh, my goodness. Now I am horny and want you so badly, Mr. Sherlock Homes. I wish you were home, Rick. I miss you badly. I'll get the dogs' ready gear on and head downtown. I love you and have your back until this nightmare is over. Please come home to us safely."

I called Jimbo back, "Boss, Kelly, is on her way with the dogs. Have them sworn in also. I don't want any mishaps or errors on taking that piece of shit Ripper down. I told you that I was going to burn the entire East Coast charter down and we're close now. I have several bigger narcotic and gun deals to do and I want to buy the C4 from the army guy. Hatchet already told me that I'd be able to buy four pounds of the C4 from Jason and Big Bear."

Jimbo said, "Okay, I'll have the SAC sign off on wiring you thirty thousand to get the deals done, and let's wrap this damn investigation up."

The team arrived at Ripper's building around 4:30 PM. They made sure that he wasn't around. Jimbo called for the manager and asked to see the maintenance man.

The maintenance worker came into the manager's office and his boss said, "Felix, these folks need to speak with you for a moment. I'll be in the break room if you need me."

Jimbo said, "Felix, do you know this man?" He showed him a photo of Ripper.

Felix said, "Sure, that's Rip. He's a cool dude. Always tips me when I do something for him."

Kelly said, "Like let him make copies of the boiler room master keys?"

Felix said, "No way. I'd never do that kind of thing. I got a good thing over here."

Kelly let Talia and Ronin's leash out another foot toward Felix. Kelly asked, "Did you give your so-called friend Rip the keys to the boiler room? Lie to me again and I'm letting them go and they'll rip your balls off then tear out your damn fucking throat."

Talia and Ronin began to growl and pull on their leashes. Felix cried out, "Okay, you got me. I gave him the master key to the boiler room. He goes down there to fuck some chicks once in a while behind his girlfriend's back."

Kelly said to her unit, "Cuff this piece of shit and bring him downtown to be processed for being in possession of cocaine and meth."

Felis screamed, "I'm clean, I don't have any drugs on me."

Kelly let go of Talia and gave her the command, "Cuardaigh (search in Irish)."

Talia grabbed Felix's leg pants and pulled him to the ground. Ronin went in for the assist to secure the perp. Talia pulled out an ounce of crank from inside the sock of his right pants leg.

Then Bryce the AUSA said, "Well, this is unbelievably bad for you Felix. That's felony possession of illegal narcotics. That's ten years in the federal penitentiary. And if you have a felony arrest, it's twenty years. You better start giving up your source by the time we leave here."

Felix said, "Man, they'll kill me if I do."

Jimbo said, "We can have the dogs give you a quick death if that's what you prefer."

Felix ranted, "Okay, okay. I'll talk, but you gotta get me somewhere safe. You already know my dealer. He lives in the building; It's Rip and I have others from his club, I can give you. But you need to get me the hell out of here."

Bryce told one of the other NYBN agents to bring him downtown to his office. Jimbo unlocked the door to the boiler room and it was spotless. The floor had been recently painted battleship grey. The dogs began to sniff the floor and surrounding areas of the room. Ronin was going crazy in the rear corner near the actual boiler itself. The agents and several members of Kelly's team began to break up the floor.

After two hours of back-breaking digging, they came up empty. Kelly let go of both dogs again and they were now barking and scratching at the cinder block wall near the boiler.

Jimbo said, "Take photos of the wall first. We'll need to put it back just like it is now. I don't want Ripper to know we were down here. Now break that fuckin wall down. Kelly, call the dogs back. I don't want them getting injured. Rick will kill me if something happens to you or the dogs."

It took several swings of the sledgehammers to break through the wall. Jimbo shined his mag light into the hole in the wall. He said. "Holy mother of God there's at least four bodies in there and they're wrapped up in cellophane."

The smell of decaying corpses filled the air instantly. Jimbo said, "Tear down the entire damn wall. Everyone put the Vicks Vapor Rub under your nose. Agent Neary, pour out the DOA crystals to dampen that fucking putrid smell."

By the time the wall had been taken down, they'd recovered eight bodies in total. One corpse had been beheaded. Six were young women in their mid to late teens. The other two were young men in their late teens or early twenties. The NYPD CSI team came in, fingerprinted each body, and sent the prints over to their lab to get positive identifications on the victims. The NYBN construction crew came in next and reconstructed the wall to look as it had before the team had arrived.

Back at the downtown office Kelly texted me and wrote, "He killed eight people and cut the head off of one of the victims. Six young women and two males. Ripper is done. Get these deals finalized and get the hell out of there. It's time to come home. We won't go after Ripper until you're through making your buys. Just get them done. It's getting way out of hand. Kahuna will meet you at a disclosed location where it's safe for both of you. He'll text you at 8:00 PM tonight. I love

XV

Treasurer

Two weeks after the discovery of the bodies, Hatchet had had enough of the absent Riddler and announced that he was out bad.

At church that Thursday he said, "Riddler is out bad and Rogue is the new treasurer. He's got the brains and knows how to keep his shit together and I'm sure he'll do the same for our chapter. All in agreement raise your hands."

The entire table raised their hands and I was told to grab the ledger and record the rest of the meeting. Hatchet handed me a rectangle patch that read Treasurer. I sat on the right side next to Hatchet across from Whippet. Now I would have all the evidence I needed to complete the RICO Act. I'd have the members paying dues and giving the Mother club payments for the crimes they were involved in. The final nail was being driven into the chapter's coffin.

By April of 2023, I'd taken photos of the entire ledger and also committed it to memory. The AUSA Bryce Cobb was working night and day to file petitions for the search and arrest warrants of the Brooklyn and East Coast chapters. Meanwhile, I was now so deep into the club that I was conducting narcotic buys from the New Jersey, Boston, and Pennsylvania chapters.

I'd set up three buys for large quantities of narcotics from all three in the same week. First came the Jersey chapter. I met up with Chang the VP, Dante their Treasurer, and Terry the Sergeant at Arms. Chang slipped me a note under the table at the diner we were eating at.

It said, "The cost for three pounds of crank is $4500,00. Dante and Terry have a few guns and some bulletproof vests for sale also."

I had close to $15000.00 on me so, I wrote back.

"How much for everything? "Hatchet has a strong feeling the Marquis is planning on making a move on the Brooklyn chapter. I need to be ready for anything."

Chang whispered into Dante's ear and said to me, "$10,000 for everything brother. You get the Excalibur discount."

We went outside and I asked to see the merchandise. Terry opened up the trunk of his beat-up Chevy Malibu. Dante pulled a green wool cover off a box. Inside were two bulletproof vests, four sawed-off shotguns, three Glock 19s, and one tech-nine machine gun which they had converted to a fully automatic machine gun. And on top was the three pounds of crank.

I took a quick look around to make sure no one was in the area. In reality, I was checking to see if the three of them were armed while conducting the deal. Sure, enough each one of them was packing Glocks in their waistbands. That added an additional ten years for engaging in narcotic and gun deals while being armed convicted felons. I knew all of them had served two separate stints in prison on felony charges. Three more knuckleheads would be going away for life.

I was disappointed in the fact I couldn't convince them to travel to New York to conduct business. If they had done so, they would have been charged with being in possession of illegal firearms and felony weight of narcotics while crossing state lines. Hopefully, I could get either the Boston or Pennsylvania chapter to conduct business in Brooklyn somewhere.

I handed Hatchet two thousand dollars for allowing me to do the deal. He asked, "Hey Rogue what the fuck are you doing with all this crank anyway? Did you start doing that shit?"

"Hatch, you know how many tweakers that ride bikes come into the store? They're always asking me if I know anyone selling. Plus, I have the stolen bike and parts gig going in the back of the shop. The Centurions are proving to be my best customers for that gig. They steal other bikers' hogs while they're parked in front of bars. I buy shit from them all the time. Come by the shop tomorrow and I'll show you what I mean. Maybe you'll want to buy one of the bikes I rebuilt. Your bike is going to die any day brother. I'll sell you one of them for two grand. I normally get five to seven for the bikes I rebuild. But you're my Pres. and good friend."

Hatchet said, "Fucking ay, I see you around 1:00 in the afternoon."

The Centurions were selling me parts from Harleys and had sold me five brand new 2023 Street Glides right out of a Harley shop in East Islip, New York. Those bikes go from anywhere between $21,000.00 to $27,000.00.

Keg the Sergeant at Arms, Hoodlum, Misfit, Vamp, and Doberman their President had each sold me a bike for three grand a piece. Those dim whits had no idea what the bikes were worth. They just needed to feed their addiction.

In May of 2023, the Boston chapter agreed to come out to Brooklyn as long as I brought them lunch at Denny's. I had told them they could eat as much as they wanted to. Borden the President, Scout, the VP, and Bronson the Sergeant at Arms came through the Denny's restaurant and joined me in the booth I was sitting at.

This deal was much larger. It was strictly for narcotics. Borden had gotten his hands on fifty pounds of crank and was willing to sell it to me for thirty-five thousand. It took a lot of wheeling and dealing from Jimbo to get the buy money. Especially when the head honcho's in Washington, DC wanted to shut down the case a half a year ago. The SAC, Jacob Sharp told Jimbo I had three weeks left and he was pulling me out.

We ate pancakes and waffles and a shit load of bacon. I downed four cups of coffee and slid a vanilla envelope that contained thirty-five grand across the table to Borden

Scout said, "Follow me to the back of the parking lot. The shit is in the van. I seal-wrapped it for you."

I saw that he had a 9mm beretta tucked behind his back as he went to open the rear doors of the van. Scout was a monster of a man. He could have been a professional bodybuilder if he had wanted to. Instead, he lived the life of an outlaw biker. He was heavily tattooed with prison tats. His front upper teeth were all gold--capped. To be honest he was a very intimidating person.

I said, "Let me get my ride and I'll park in the space next to you."

I drove my AMX over and we loaded the drugs into my trunk. Borden and Bronson came out and we shook hands. They both had what appeared to be 357 Magnums tucked inside their waistbands. The barrels were short so it was more than likely they had Smith and Wesson Model 19s on them.

I kept thinking to myself, "Shit I'm not wearing a vest and if one of them pulls out and shoots me, I'm not getting back up. Those revolvers are powerful and will blow a hole straight through my chest and back. I need to get this deal done and get the fuck out of here."

Borden said, "We need to head back to Boston, Rogue. I left a fifty on the table and told the waitress you'll be back to pay the tab."

I said, "Sounds good Pres. Pleasure doing business with you all. See you at the poker run next month. Drive safe."

They drove off and I waited a few minutes to call Jimbo. When Scout was grabbing the narcotics I'd hit the back tail light to make the directional signal bulb pop loose. As I hit the light I told Scout that the van was perfect for long runs. So, he just thought I was checking the van's body out.

I called Jimbo on my UC phone. "Hey Jimbo, have a NYPD patrol car pick them up. Their license plate number is as follows. Massachusetts plates HCR1296. They're all armed heavily. I'd have them call for a backup unit once they stop them. You never know what those crazy fuckers will do. Once they have them bring their asses to a black site and no fucking phone calls or flipping these guys. I'm not asking Jimmy. If any of the agents attempt to flip one of them. I'd be made and executed on the spot. Also, I had a meeting with Kahuna and he's planning something that will draw the big dogs out of their cages. I'll fill you in when I get all the details from him.

Twenty minutes later, right before Borden and his guys were stopped and handcuffed by the NYPD Highway Patrol who pulled them over. He called it in and asked for backup from the State Police. The patrolman and his partner approached the van cautiously and told the driver, who was Scout, to show them his hands and turn off the vehicle.

Scout complied and was told to step out of the van. In the meantime, a State Trooper came onto the scene to back them up. The officer asked Scout, "Do you know why I stopped you, sir?"

Scout said, "No, I have no idea officer."

The officer said, "When you changed lanes you didn't signal."

Scout yelled, "The fuck I didn't you fucking lying pig."

With that Scout was instantly tasered and Borden and Bronson were held at gunpoint and ordered out of the vehicle. They were also cuffed and the state police and the NYPD began the in plain view search which is always stretched into a regular search of a vehicle. The three weapons were recovered along with two more pounds of crank and the thirty-five thousand dollars of buy money.

Jimbo called the NYPD and had them deliver the suspects to the downtown seedy motel off of the Westside Highway. They would be held there until the investigation was completed. We had arrest warrants on all the members that had been taken into custody. They were charged with being in possession of a firearm while committing a violent felony, first-degree narcotics sales, drug trafficking, drug distribution, and possession of deadly firearms. Also, crossing state lines while being in possession of felony weight. Everything was beginning to fall into place. The three Boston members were now facing 40 years in federal prison.

In between all the buys with the other chapters I was making gun and narcotic buys from my own club, the support clubs, The Centurions, and The Crypt Keepers. I started buying pounds of crank and ounces of cocaine from Blade, Steel, and Jason. Guardrail had also sold me ten grams of fentanyl. I had every member in my club on countless felony charges that would give them all at least twenty years in prison. The Treasurer and VP of the Crypt Keepers sold me fifty grams of fentanyl and two more stolen Harleys. The last chapter to get was the Pennsylvania chapter and that would be the most dangerous one of all.

In the meantime, while I was waiting to do the deal with the PA chapter, 45 had agreed to sell me two pounds of C4 explosives for five grand. I told him I needed it to blow up some scumbag's house in Maine. I found out the guy was fucking my girlfriend on the side. I was going to blow up his house and her house all on the same day.

45 said, "Bro, that's some heavy shit you're going through. If you need to talk to someone. I'm always here for you. I'll even deliver the Christmas presents for you and do the deed myself if you need me to."

I said, "Thanks brother, but I can get in and out of there much quicker than you and set the bombs in the right places outside their houses to do the most damage and make sure there are no survivors. I got this bro. But thanks, and I'm okay with this shit. Fuck there's plenty of pussy out there for me to bang."

I'd purchased the two pounds of C4 the next day from 45 and now had his ass for selling me high-grade explosives and conspiracy to commit murder.

Hatchet already had plunged the dagger in his heart when he participated in the rape of a 21-year girl at the Cove a few months back. Thank God I had left early that night.

When I saw a couple going into the club I thought it was strange that a guy would bring his girl to a strip club. But I really didn't think about much after that. Whippet had told me the next day how they pummeled the boyfriend because his girl was hitting on Hatchet and her boyfriend went over to confront Hatchet about it. The guy made the mistake of poking Hatchet in the chest and grabbing his colors. That was a big No, No. Blade and Steel beat the living shit out of the guy and he died three days later. They plunged their axes into his chest and back.

The girl had a train run on her by five members of the Excaliburs. (A train is when several members of an OMG take turns having sex with a woman). The victim wasn't a willing participant in the train ride. Hatchet had gotten so into choking her that he ended up killing the woman and her body was dumped somewhere in a Hunting preserve out in the Hamptons. They figured wild animals would eat the dead woman before anyone could discover her. That was their second mistake of that night. I phoned Jimbo to get some hunters and the preserve people to comb the area for the woman. That way it wouldn't look like I had ratted Whippet and the others out.

I knew that the PA deal would be the last component of the investigation. By then Bryce would have all the arrest and search warrants sworn out. He'd also convince the judge to allow him to do forty sealed indictments. All of the indictments were presented to jurors in five different districts and all came back with true bills. The Excaliburs were all going away for an exceptionally long time.

The last deal was set for early June of 2023 with the PA chapter. Dayton, the president of the PA chapter, set a date in mid-June to meet me with 100 hundred grams of Fentanyl and a kilo of cocaine.

I picked the same Denny's in Brooklyn. Dayton, Mayo the VP, and Marcus, one of their enforcers walked into the Denny's and we exchanged handshakes then sat down and ordered a big breakfast. These three members were gigantic. Each of them weighed at least two hundred and fifty pounds or more. And they could eat. They ordered over $200.00 worth of pancakes, waffles, bacon, steak, and eggs. I just had an order of waffles, two eggs, and a side of bacon with plenty of butter and syrup. The waitress kept the coffee flowing too.

After we were done eating I paid the bill and tipped her a hundred dollars to let us stay and drink coffee for a little while.

Marcus said, "You have the money, Rogue?"

I said, "Yes, right here next to me in this gym bag. Did you bring what I ordered?"

Mayo said, "Hold on there, bud, we haven't settled on a price yet."

I said, "Okay, then let's get to it. It's getting late and I have a nice piece of ass waiting for me at my pad."

Mayo said, "Nice, sounds good. Okay for the Fentanyl it's going to be ten grand. The kilo will cost you twenty-three grand. You good with that, brother?"

I went into the bag, counted out the thirty-three thousand, and placed it into a large brown paper shopping bag.

I said. "Thirty-three K. You can count it if you'd like, but maybe do it in your car.

Dayton said, "No it's all good, Rogue. Let's go to our ride and get you your shit."

Marcus opened the trunk, opened a brown leather bag, and showed me the narcotics. I took the bag and we said our goodbyes. I told Jimbo to let them go back to PA and we would take them down when we hit all the other members' doors in the coming months. Those three sleaze balls were facing twenty to forty years in prison.

Hatchet asked me if it would be okay to hold church at my house the following Thursday after I'd completed the PA deal. He also had come into the shop and purchased the stolen 2023 Street Glide from me for three thousand. The case was coming to an end and the techs had been to my UC pad and made sure all the recording and audio equipment was working properly. They made sure that no devices could be seen or heard while we recorded the church meeting.

Church was held and sure enough Big Bear used a wand to check for wires and bugs. The jammers that the techs installed blocked everything from being detected. I had the video running and the audio rolling for the past half hour. We were good for up to eight hours of taping.

Hatchet called the meeting to start and I called roll call and logged in everyone present. I then collected the dues and sealed them up in a white envelope.

Hatchet was in a foul mood and said, "Listen up, we're down four members and I'm getting word from the lawyers Jason, Steele, Blade, and myself may have to go on the lamb for a bit for the untimely deaths of the two fuckers, and bitch we did. So, before that happens, we're going to be on a search and snatch mission of a certain member of the Guardians. He's the VP and he goes by the club name Kahuna.

That's the mother fucker who grabbed Riddler on the bail bond. Those mother fuckers are collecting bounties off of a lot of OMGs. So, now it's payback time. I'm waiting for the P. I. to get me the location of this Kahuna and then we'll kidnap him and bring that scumbag to the place to deliver some real justice. If I'm going to jail. I might as well send one of the Guardians to the grave first. I'll give you all the details in a few days via text messages. Have your phones on at all times. This meeting is adjourned. Rogue go outside and burn the minutes of this meeting."

I said, "10-4 Pres."

XVI

Title Shot

After church was held the members left the UC pad. I took the tapes out of the recorders and met with Jimbo and handed them over to him. I also informed him of what the Excaliburs were planning to do to Kahuna. I also stressed to him that the Excaliburs were getting ready to plant the C4 at several clubhouses of rival OMGs. In particular the Guardian's and the Marquis's. And I would be the one conducting those operations.

Jimbo said, "Listen brother, we're in this together. It's just you and me now. I'd like to get Kelly assigned to me and be your other cover vehicle for backup. I want her to bring the dogs with her at all times. Are you good with that?"

"Where the fuck did Beck, go now?"

Jimbo took a deep breath, "She was called in to conduct a long undercover operation against one of the cartel factions in Washington Heights. Nothing I could do about it. The order came down from D.C. We're on our own for the remainder of this operation. I have your six."

I said, "If Kelly's good with it. So am I. Let's just wrap this nightmare up. I want to go home to my wife and kids. I miss them. I feel like I'm one of these bastards now, to be honest with you. I feel like the job has betrayed me. All of them except you. If it wasn't for you and Kelly. I'd be going dark and joining up with the Guardians. Those guys have more honor than anyone in the bureau."

The next few weeks I was knee-deep into doing my treasury duties for the club. I had every one of the chapters making narcotics sales, buying guns from major arms dealers, and reselling the merchandise to me and other club members. The Boston, Brooklyn, and Manhattan chapters were all going away for dealing and plotting to use the C4 high-grade explosives. (18 U.S.C. § 845).

Arthur and his VP Lancelot came down to our clubhouse to meet with me and Hatchet to discuss the details of using the bombs to blow up the Guardians, and Marquis clubhouses.

Arthur said, "Rogue I want these operations done with precision and you can use one other member to assist you in the operation. I want to see it on the news that both of their clubhouses are blown up into pieces. I don't give a fuck if women or children are inside the clubhouses. Just get it done and be ready to be called on to administer some punishment to that fucking shithead Kahuna. He's going down tomorrow night. The other officers of the Mother Chapter will be here later for your scheduled church meeting and then to party so, let's get to drinking."

I said, "I'll start making the necessary plans to attack them now, Arthur. Thank you, for this great honor to take those fuckers out."

I left the clubhouse and headed to my UC pad. Then I called Kelly, Jimbo, and Uncle Bobby on a three-way call to inform them to have Kahuna be on the lookout."

Uncle Bobby said, "Rick, Kahuna has been advised of everything and is making the necessary plans to take the Excaliburs out for good. The Guardians have Jimbo's and Kelly's backs from here on in. I have to stay neutral in regards to any retaliation."

I said, "Understood Uncle Bobby, and thanks for all the help during these past two years. I know it's been a grind on you and everyone else."

I spoke with Kelly on a private line. "Kelly, how are you holding up? And how are the kids and pups doing? We're close to the finish line baby."

Kelly said, "We're all good. The dogs and I are all ready to deliver these bastards to hell or a prison cell. Whatever the situation calls for. I'm done playing games with them and the dogs are hungry for some human blood. I won't be holding them back on this operation. Not when it comes to your safety. I want my husband back home with our kids and in my bed."

I said, "Just a few more days and this will be over. All of the warrants have been drawn up and all Jimbo needs to do is coordinate all the agencies that will be assisting in the takedown and the time it will happen. I love you always and forever babe. Put Jimbo back on for a minute please."

Kelly said, "I love you more baby, stay safe and kick their asses inside and out. Take no fucking prisoners this time."

Jimbo said, "What's up bud? How are you holding up?"

I said, "Listen I just sent over the transactions that were made by all of the chapters this week and the audio tape of Arthur ordering me to blow up the

Guardian's and Marquis's clubhouses. I have him admitting that the Excaliburs are getting ready to kidnap and murder Kahuna. They picked the wrong guy to kidnap. When you take these fuckers down. Do every state at the same time on the same day. Get me the hell out of there at least six hours before the takedown.

Something is brewing for tonight's party at the clubhouse in Brooklyn. I don't have a good feeling about it at all. But I've come this far to back out now. I'll call you when I'm back at the UC pad later tonight. Have Kelly pick up some gray modeling clay from the arts and crafts store and package it like the C4 to make it look like the real. Have her leave it under the dumpster at the Odd Lot."

Jimbo said. "That's a big 10-4 brother. Talk to you later."

At 8:00 PM Ripper and a few of the Mother Club officers came into the clubhouse. He screamed, "Mother fucker, now I know you're a cop."

With that, he charged at me, axe in hand, and took an over-the-head chop at the base of my skull. I sprang out of my chair and had my throwing axe in my right hand. Ripper's axe blade sliced downward against the top of my forehead and I blocked his powerful blow and prevented the blade from taking my left eye out. The momentum of his blade continued to cut my left lower orbital. My axe handle pushed his axe away from my face.

Big Bear sped toward Ripper and jackknifed him onto the floor. Big Bear and Guardrail held Ripper on the floor while 45 stuck his gun into Ripper's mouth.

45 said, "Suck on this, you fucking piece of shit. Rogue ain't no cop and now you're going to answer to Arthur for falsely accusing our brother of an offense that calls for your death."

Arthur, Lancelot, and Hatchet rushed into the clubhouse.

Arthur screamed, "What the fuck is going on here. Take your gun out of Ripper's mouth now 45 or I'll execute you right where you're standing."

Arthur and Lancelot pulled their guns out. 45 removed his revolver from Ripper's mouth but Guardrail and Big Bear were still holding him down.

Arthur said, "Speak now Ripper, because you've pushed me to my limits."

Ripper sat up and said, "Huntsman from the Crypt Keepers called me and told me that he observed Kahuna and the Guardians surround Riddler on I-95, throw him into their van, and sped off toward New York. Huntsman followed them all the way downtown to the office of the New York Bureau of Narcotics. While we were at the Roar at the Shore, I went to the head late at night when everyone was sleeping and I heard that mother fucking cop call out Kahuna's name while he was sleeping. Looked like he was having some kind of nightmare. He's working with the Guardians and knows that Kahuna dude."

Now Arthur and Lancelot pointed their weapons at me. Arthur said, "Well, Rogue, you want to explain yourself?"

I said, "Fuck yeah, I do. You've all seen my military file or at least some of you have. If you've ever served in a special branch of the military then you know that the team leader goes by the name, Kahuna. Better known as the Big Kahuna. He's the shot caller. I saved my team leader's life by taking much of the blast from a Claymore bomb during one of the missions I was involved in. My K9 dog was killed but I saved my team leader Kahuna's life. I have PTSD and have nightmares all the time. I probably was reliving that operation. Sorry if that lunkhead doesn't know about the military nicknames. I'm no fucking cop or rat."

Arthur was fuming and then turned his weapon back on Ripper. He said, Ripper, you're Out Bad. Remove your colors and hand over your keys to your bike. I'm done covering for you and your sick murdering ways. You've put tremendous heat on our entire club."

Ripper said, "That's fine, old man. Now I'm going to beat that fucking cop to death."

I said to Hatchet, "Can you get your heavy-duty stapler out of your office? I need to close this wound before I destroy that mother fucker."

The wound on my forehead and below my eye needed at least ten stitches. The staples would have to do for the time being. Each time I pulled the staple gun handle to release a staple into my forehead to seal the wound, every member winced at the sight of it.

After I completed the barbaric closing of the laceration, I said to Arthur and Hatchet. "Inside here or out in the lot? And what are the rules of engagement, King Arthur?"

Arthur said, "This will be a fight to the death or permanently being maimed for life. There are no rules. Now let's get it on."

They released Ripper and tore off his colors. We walked out to the parking lot and the members put their headlights on to brighten the area.

I walked up to Ripper and said, "Hey Bub, you want *a Shot at the Title?*"

Ripper threw a haymaker punch at me and I ducked. When I came up I sent a violent right uppercut punch to the bottom of his chin. (It's called a cigarette punch because the person's mouth is open during the fight. They don't know how to breathe through their nose while they're in a fight. They breathe through their mouths instead to get more air.) His bottom teeth collided with his top teeth. I sent a left uppercut to his chin as his head came back down from snapping back. His teeth rattled again and now his bottom and two top front teeth were loose. He shook the cobwebs out and landed a solid punch to my ribs. I knew he'd cracked at least two of them.

He spat blood in my direction and missed. He charged me and placed me into a bear hug. I tucked out of it and grabbed his left arm and snapped it in half at the elbow. He screamed in pain. He aimlessly swung a roundhouse punch at me with his right fist. I blocked the punch with my forearm and his forearm fractured immediately. His arms dangled and I grabbed his right hand and pulled it upward snapping his wrist. Then snapped his right arm in half at that elbow. I sent two vicious front kicks right below each kneecap and broke both of his legs. Both legs had compound fractures and the bones were sticking out.

Ripper crumbled to the ground. The Brooklyn Chapter cheered me on to finish him. As he was on the ground I did a front mount and grabbed him by his ear and sent smashing headbutts into his eyes and nose.

I leaned into his right ear and whispered, "You were right from the start. I am an undercover agent."

He went to yell out what I had just said to him and I sent my right elbow into his jaw and shattered it on the right side. He was mumbling but no one could understand him.

I leaned into his left ear and said, "I know all about the eight bodies you hid behind the cinder blocks in the boiler room of your building. You know the six teenage girls one of them that you beheaded, and those two young men. Looks like you still had a taste for some of that man ass that you were fucking in prison. How about we see what the King and your old friends behind me think about you being a homosexual? You're going away for life mother fucker."

Ripper tried in vain to tell Arthur I'd just admitted to being a cop. I sent my left elbow into the left side of his jaw and shattered that side.

His jaw dropped from its hinges and dangled helplessly. Ripper passed out from the pain. I looked at Arthur to see if he was going to run his thumb across his neck or give the thumb up to let Ripper live.

Arthur said, "It's up to you Rogue, do what you want to do with that piece of shit. Wake him up first I have something I need to say to this scumbag."

45 threw me a bottle of beer and I poured it onto Ripper's face. He tried to open his swollen eyes and tears rolled out of them.

Arthur said, Excaliburs, I have kept a horrible secret from you all, to protect this stupid no good piece of shit. This man is a fucking faggot and likes to fuck men. I followed him one night to Penn Station and watched this maggot pick up two young men and drive them to his apartment building. I'm guilty of not reporting this cock sucker's vile habits to the club. At the time he was a huge asset to our club. I will give my resignation in tomorrow if you want me to."

Hatchet said, "There's no need for you to do that, Arthur. You were just protecting the club. Am I right, brothers?"

We all agreed to keep Arthur as the Mother Chapter President until his term was up the following year.

I then said, "Throw Ripper into the street like the rest of the garbage and maybe someone will show him mercy and bring him to a hospital. No one from the Excaliburs is to take him to the emergency room. He gets there himself. He made his bed. Now he can sleep in it."

Arthur said, "First duct tape his head and entire face. Cut a hole in the mouth area so he breathe. Wherever you dump his ass, duct tape him to a utility pole, and then call 911. Make sure you use a burner phone when you're calling 911."

Lancelot said, "Fuck, Rogue, remind me never to get on your bad side. You're fucking insane."

45 and Big Bear took me to one of the club's underground doctors to get me properly stitched up. I was advised by Hatchet that the snatch and grab would be the following Friday. With the turn of events with Ripper, Arthur needed to elect a new Sergeant at Arms before any moves were made.

I asked Hatchet if I could have the night off to heal up. Hatchet said, "You, fucking earn it. Go rest and get laid. See you this Thursday. You'll be setting the C4 in the enemies' clubhouses. Go rest up brother."

I called Jimbo to let him know what had transpired. He said, "Rick, you need to do that big buy for the C4 with Kendrick before Tuesday. We're working with the Special Investigator from the 101 to finalize the arrest. Kendrick will be court-martialed right after you do the buy. Get that deal done and let's put the rest of these bastards to bed for good."

I said, "Okay I'm going home for the next few days to spend some time with Kelly."

When I arrived home, Kelly's eyes widened and she had tears in them. She said, "My God, what have they done to you? What the hell happened to your face? You look like you were in a damn war."

I said, "Ripper is done. I fought him in a death match but let him live. He'll be a quadriplegic for the rest of his life. I snapped his arms in half and made sure the tendons and ligaments were severed. I did the same to his legs with front snap kicks that sent his kneecaps through the back of his legs. You and I will be visiting him in whatever hospital he goes to and I'm going to end him for good. He's not seeing a courtroom. I'm sending that scumbag to hell where he belongs. He doesn't deserve to breathe the air other humans breathe"

Kelly said, "Come here my love, and let me take care of you. Can I tell you something? That's going to leave a nasty scar. But damn. it does make you look even hotter than you already are. You know me and scars. I love that you have them. You're a damn warrior and you're mine forever. You're my Spartan warrior, Rick Volpe.

XVII

The Take Down

During the two-year investigation, I'd been able to purchase large amounts of narcotics, guns, and C4. To put the icing on the cake we had several of the Excaliburs on murder charges and the entire club on conspiracy charges. A total of forty sealed indictments were handed down. (That's when the grand jury is convened in secret and a sealed indictment is held without the subject's knowledge). The Excaliburs were walking around like they owned the world and had no idea they were going away for life. Most of the members on the East Coast had two prior felony convictions and were facing the three-strike deal.

On July 28, 2023, I called Kendrick and put in an order for fifty pounds of C4 with the detonating devices. Kendrick said, "Mr. Rick, you ready to blow some mother fuckers up? I have the shit and can meet you tonight at the Viena Diner in Queens. Are you interested in some hand grenades I have ten ready to do their thing do you want them?"

I said, "Fucking Ay, I want them too."

Kendrick said, "All the goods will cost you $25,000.00. The heat is on me and I have two weeks until I'm honorably discharged."

I said, "Twenty-Five K. Come on, Kendrick. I'll give you $22,000.00 and that's my final offer."

There was silence on the phone then he said, "Done deal. Meet me at the diner at 9:00 PM tonight. Come alone, Rick, and don't be stupid and think you can do a rip on me. I'll have eyes all over that place."

I said, "No worries Kendrick, I'll be alone."

Jimbo and Kelly had heard and recorded the entire conversation and were making the necessary calls to grab Kendrick with the 101 Special Investigator unit from the Army. I called General Walton and advised him when the deal would be taking place.

General Walton said, "Great job Rick, I'll have my guys in place. They have your back. You, good if we take over after the arrest? He's our boy and needs to be court-martialed immediately. I don't want some JAG lawyer feeding him bullshit to say. If I need to, I'll bring his ass to (GTMO) Guantanamo Bay myself. That little shithead needs to pay for this act of terrorism. Rick if he even makes one false move. You have the green light to eradicate the threat immediately.

I said, "10-4 General. Thanks again for the backup."

I told Hatchet I needed to work extra overtime for the shop and wouldn't be around that night. He had told me to make myself available and ready to do the snatch-and-grab on Kahuna that Thursday night.

I needed to meet with Uncle Bobby and Kahuna in the morning. I sent them both text messages with the location for the meet. I chose the Merrick Diner on Merrick Road. It was a secluded eatery and we wouldn't be bothered. I also told Kahuna to drive his car. I wrote "No bikes just in case one of the Excaliburs or Centurions ride by. I also wrote, "No Colors."

I arrived at the Viena diner at 7:30 PM and ordered coffee and a toasted blueberry muffin just to kill time and take the edge off my nerves. This was an extremely dangerous buy and bust and one wrong move by any of the personnel that was working the operation could be catastrophic. Kendrick drove into the parking lot right on time and was sitting on the rear bumper of his black Jeep Wrangler.

I said, "Evening friend. How's things going at the Fort."

Kendrick said, "Things are things, bro. You got the money?"

I opened my duffle bag and showed him the cash. I said, "Twenty-two grand, sir. Where's the merchandise?"

Kendrick opened the back door to the Jeep and pulled a green Army blanket off a wooden crate that had the fifty pounds of C4, the detonating devices, and the ten hand grenades. I handed him the duffle bag, carefully picked up the crate, and placed it into the trunk of my car. We shook hands and went our separate ways. The deal went down so smoothly it was scary. Kendrick was apprehended on the Belt Parkway right before the exit to Fort Hamilton.

The Special Investigator of the 101 took Kendrick into custody without incident. General Walton was extremely pleased with the outcome of the undercover operation. He texted me that he was putting me in for a medal.

Next, I went home to spend the rest of the night with Kelly and the kids. As always it was a magical evening. Kelly cooked an amazing baked ziti and meatballs and we ate a double feature of dessert. Chocolate cake and cheesecake surrounded by Reese's Peanut Butter Cups. That night Kelly and I went at each other like two savages in heat.

We laid down in our bed and I asked her, "Love, are you up for a covert operation that I haven't cleared with anyone involved in the case? It would be just you and I who are involved. But if we were to get caught it would mean the kids would be raised by your parents."

Kelly asked, "Are you saying you want to kill someone?"

I said, "I'm going to finish Ripper in the morning. I'm heading to the hospital and will sneak into his room and send his pathetic ass to hell. I already have what I need but I need a diversion to get the nurses and doctors out of the area where he's being treated."

Kelly looked at the ceiling for several minutes and turned and looked right into my eyes.

She said, "That shithead doesn't deserve to live. I say we do it and hope for the best but expect the worst if something comes out of it."

I said, "I'll make sure that it's me that takes the fall if it comes down to it. You're just a diversion. I'm thinking you can sneak into another patient's room on the opposite wing of the floor that Ripper is on. Pull a cord that just sends a false cardiac arrest signal. Just make sure not to cut the person's oxygen. We don't want an innocent person getting hurt."

Kelly said, "I know what to do and it will be an easy slip in and out of the room. Now speaking of slipping in and out. I'm ready for round two. But make this one last for a long time, mister. Momma bear has missed Pappa bear a lot."

The next morning Kelly's sister picked up the kids and we ate breakfast, showered, and headed to the Metropolitan Hospital in Manhattan. We walked in very casually and I checked around to see if any of the Excaliburs were going in to visit Ripper against Arthur's back.

The floor where Ripper was had no signs of OMGs on it. Kelly went to the West Wing of the hospital and I went to the East Wing where Ripper's room was. I waited for my wife to go into action. Within two minutes a code blue was called on the West Wing of the floor and nurses and doctors were flying toward the area. I saw Kelly take the stairs down and head back to the car. I stepped into Ripper's room and he tried to scream out.

I said, "Now, Lance, buddy, let's just stop the crying and get this over with."

Ripper was crying and mumbled for me to spare his life.

I said, "Hey, mother fucker you fucked with the wrong wolf. Now it's time to answer for all those innocent people you raped and murdered. I'm sending you to hell and no one will ever know I was here. Say goodnight cock sucker"

With that I injected several air bubbles into his IV and within a minute he started to convulse and his eyes began to bulge out. I snuck out of the room but stayed in the area to hear the long beep of a flatline on his breathing machine. He was dead and no longer a menace to society. I cautiously walked to the car unnoticed and Kelly sped out of the garage and back to our house. We had a drink to decompress.

Hatchet was blowing up my phone and telling me to get my ass over to the clubhouse. He said, "Where the fuck have you been, Rogue? When I call, you better get your fucking ass over here ASAP."

I said, "It won't happen again, Pres."

Hatchet smirked and said, "Damn skippy it won't happen again. Now go into the van and get the six Christmas presents (C4) and the devices. Your mission begins now. Plant the presents at the Guardian's clubhouse in Manhattan. Their clubhouse is on the West Side Highway and 56th Street. Be careful over there. We just obtained intel that those fuckers are being backed by the Westies. You'll be going into Hell's Kitchen and it could prove to be very hostile. Take your car instead of your bike and go in civilian clothes.

After you've planted the presents in their clubhouse, move onto Astoria, Queens at 120th and Main Street. You'll see Edmunds Motorcycle Shop on the corner. The Marquis's clubhouse is in the back of the shop. Plant the other three Christmas presents in their clubhouse. And get the fuck out of dodge.

Meet us at the place around 1:00 AM. We'll have the package there and you're going to torture that mother fucker Kahuna to death. That's Arthur's order. I think he's still a bit pissed that you mangled Ripper. He was his best soldier."

I said, "Too fucking bad for Arthur. I did as I was told and followed the rules of the pit and his words to the letter. I could have killed that motherfucker."

Hatchet said, "By the way Arthur, was notified that Ripper went into cardiac arrest earlier today and is dead. You got your fucking payback good, brother. Now go make me proud and be ready for some ass-kicking tonight."

I raced out of the clubhouse and headed straight for the Odd Lot to grab the fake C4 and switch it out with the real C4 to be processed and taken back to Fort Hamilton. Once I had retrieved the molding clay I drove over to the Guardian's clubhouse. I needed to alert Kahuna that the timeframe was moved up to that night. I placed the gray clay into the spots of the clubhouse and clipped the wires so no electric sparks could ignite. I texted Kahuna, Uncle Bobby, Jimbo, and Kelly to meet me over there ASAP.

Once we were all there I had to speak fast and get to the point and give out the assignments to the team. Kahuna would handle the Guardians and give them their assignments.

I said to Kahuna. "Hey brother, it's time to collect on that favor from the Dogs of War. We need them here pronto. You can give them all the details. We need them to come in with stealth and fury."

Kahuna said, "10-4, Rogue, they'll be here and so will the Guardians ."

I threw him a small beige tracking device to blend into his skin. I said, "Put that somewhere on your body so the teams can monitor your exact location. I wasn't given the location of the place so the tracer will have to do it."

I told Kelly to prepare Talia and Ronin for the takedown. They would be suited up in vests and ready to tear apart whoever Kelly or I commanded them to. The dummy Christmas presents were in position. I said my goodbyes to everyone.

I took Kelly to the side and said, "This is it, my love. We're at the homestretch. It's kill or be killed for me. Always remember that I love you more than anything in the world. You and the kids are my world. If I don't make it. I promise I will find you in the next life and I'll say these words to you. "Love Never To End For All Eternity."

Kelly looked into my eyes and said, "You listen to me, right now. You're going to make it out alive and we'll be having dinner with the kids and dogs tomorrow night. Do you hear me, Rick Volpe? Say it."

"I hear you loud and clear. Don't hesitate for a second to put any of those fuckers down if I put up the hand signal. I love you and good luck babe."

I drove over to Astoria Queens and found the Marquis's clubhouse with no problem. For some reason, it was locked up and no one was around. That made my job much easier. I slipped into a back window, and planted the dummy Christmas presents and took photos as proof that they were put into the right areas of the clubhouse. I had done the same at the Guardian's clubhouse in Manhattan.

I drove back to Excalibur clubhouse and was greeted by Whippet and he gave me the directions of the place which turned out to be an abandoned warehouse with plenty of skylights. It was in Brooklyn near The Kings Plaza Mall. We had a beer and went over the plans for the abduction of Kahuna. I told Whippet I was going to get my supplies at my pad and would be back in thirty minutes.

I checked the wire on my cigarette lighter to make sure Jimbo and Kelly had heard the entire conversation and recorded it. I texted Kahuna the location where they'd be taking him. He in turn alerted the Guardians and the Dogs of War team who were made up of ex-Rangers, Seals, and Special Forces. All of them rode Harleys and kept close ties to Kahuna and myself. We did several missions together while in and out of the military.

While I rode back to the clubhouse I kept thinking to myself. "The Guardians are the kind of club I'd want to be a part of if I make it out of this nightmare alive."

I felt betrayed by the NYBN who would not be assisting us in the final stages of my mission. Tomorrow morning members of the NYBN, several federal agencies, and police departments will be kicking in the doors of 100-plus members of the Excaliburs, Centurions, and Crypt Keepers. It'll go down as the largest undercover operation against an OMG in history.

I met up with 45, Blade, and Jason. The others went out on the abduction of Kahuna. I felt two quick vibrations in my UC phone. That was the code for all is good and all units were at their stations. Kahuna was waiting to be grabbed at his house. At 11:30 PM we were texted by Hatchet that they had the package and we were to meet them at the place. I arrived with 45, and Jason first. Blade took the rear and kept watch for any Guardians or cops that might be on our tail. Which I knew there wasn't any. They were already hiding in the shadows waiting for the signal to pounce.

We arrived at the building and I scoped out the area to ascertain that it was all clear. I made a quick swipe of my forehead to let the teams know I was on the set. The code for the teams to make the entry of the warehouse would be two clicks of my lighter.

Arthur said, "Well, well, look what the cat dragged in. Nice job with the Christmas presents. What time are they set to go off, Rogue?"

I said, "4:00 AM when they're all sleeping."

With Arthur, there was Frenchy the Treasurer, Brute an Enforcer, Lancelot, and the Secretary, Sevenfold. From the Jersey chapter was Brooks the President, Chang the VP, and Terry the Sergeant at Arms, The Brooklyn chapter were Blade, 45, Jason, Hatchet, Big Bear, and Whippet. I counted the heads and this was going to be one hell of a firefight if things got out of hand. I only had my 9mm and one of my government-issued 380 automatics with me and my throwing axe. All of the Excaliburs had their hand-held axes and sidearms. This could become a damn bloodbath and I sure in hell didn't want my wife or the dogs in the middle of it. I needed to get to Kahuna, free him, and slip the 380 in his hands.

Arthur called me over to him and Hatchet. He said, "Okay military man. Let's see how you do some torturing of a hostile enemy."

I said, "Fucking ay right, Pres. Let me double-check his zip ties to make sure they're secure. I don't want this fucker moving while I cut him up into pieces."

I went over to Kahuna and grabbed him from behind his shoulders and said. "I'm going to enjoy this, you fucking scumbag. I bent down behind him and dropped a little acid onto the zip tie cuffs to melt the plastic. Then I placed the 380 into his hands. I made my way around to the front and surveyed the positions of all the members of the Excaliburs three on the left, five on the right sides of Kahuna and me. Hatchet and Arthur were standing behind me.

Arthur said, "Get to dicing, Rogue."

I looked at Kahuna, pulled out my throwing axe, and said, "You ready Boss?"

Kahuna said, "Let's get it on Rogue." Arthur screamed, "Do him now. That's an order or I'll fucking execute both of you right here."

I winked at Kahuna and said to Arthur. "I don't think so mother fucker."

Arthur drew his revolver and I turned and threw my axe right in the direction of his head. It landed right between his eyes. He dropped to the floor and Kahuna broke the zip ties and pulled the 380 out. I clicked my zippo lighter twice to alert the teams to come through the doors. Several members of the Guardians came crashing through the doors on their bikes. The skylights above us came crashing down. The Dogs of War slid down their black rappelling ropes and trained their weapons on the Excaliburs. Kelly and the dogs walked into the building. She was holding Talia on the right and Ronin on the left. I looked over at her and she released both dogs who ran over to my side.

Hatchet screamed, "What the fuck is this, Rogue?"

"Hatchet, you, and all of these low-life motherfuckers are under arrest. I'm a NYBN federal agent. Now throw down your weapons, slide them across the floor, and place your hands on top of your heads.

I gave a command to the dogs in Italian, "Vai alla mamma."(Go to mamma).

The dogs retreated to Kelly who was holding a Heckler & Koch MP5 submachine gun and she'd hit the selector switch to fully auto.

"Excaliburs, you're all under arrest and have already been indicted for countless felony crimes. Now this is your last warning. Drop your fucking weapons to the ground, get on your knees, and interlock to hands on your heads."

Whippet and Brooks yelled, "Go fuck yourself. You're a dead man."

Kelly had heard enough and gave Tallia the command, crotch, and tapped her left leg. That was the direction where Brooks was standing. Tallia leaped into the air and set her jaws onto Brooks' balls. Then she tapped her right leg and said in Irish, Scornach (throat). Ronin charged Whippet, jumped into the air, latched onto his throat, and tore out his vocal cords.

Jason reached behind his back for his 380 automatic and Kelly did a double tap into Jason's skull killing him instantly. The Dogs of War were getting ready to light the Excaliburs up when Hatchet gave the order to drop their weapons. Within minutes they were all put into handcuffs and taken downtown to be processed.

At 4:00 AM that morning 40 search warrants and 60 arrest warrants were successfully executed. The Excaliburs, the Centurions, and the Crypt Keepers were now in custody and their clubs were dismantled beyond repair.

The dogs and Kelly rushed over to me and we hugged for several minutes. Then Kahuna yelled over to one of the Guardians and said, "You got my brother's cut for him?" One of the members of the Guardians threw him a leather vest.

Kahuna said, "Rogue, we'd be honored if you'd ride with us. You're a fully patched member. We voted on it several nights ago. No prospecting at all. You're in if you want to be."

I said, "I'll need a few days to think about that. I'm still a federal agent and I'm not too sure how the agency will look upon that. I want to thank you all for having my family's back during this operation. I'm indebted to you for the rest of my life."

Jimbo came over to me and asked, "How are you holding up bud? The warrants were executed and all subjects were captured and detained. Thirty-five of the search warrants recovered weapons, all kinds of narcotics, and seven more bombs. The agency is ecstatic and wants a briefing in the morning."

I said, "Tell them to fuck off. I'm taking my vacation time first to be with my family. I want to clean up and eat dinner with my family and Uncle Bobby. I'll come in after my vacation is up. If they have a problem with that they can go fuck themselves. See you in a few days and make sure those turncoats from the two cover teams are nowhere near the building when I enter it."

I looked over to Kelly who was speaking with Kahuna and said, "Let's get the hell out of here."

Ronin and Talia ran over me and took their protection positions while we walked back to the AMX. One week later Uncle Bobby threw a barbecue that would go down in history in the back parking lot of his store. Representatives from all the Guardians were in attendance. I showed up in my Guardian cut. I was now a patched member of their club.

EPILOGUE

The following Excaliburs were charged and either pled guilty or were convicted of the crimes listed below at trial: Charles Hatcher (Hatchet), Scott Kem (45), Wesley Davis (Guardrail), Antonio Hudson (Blade), Eugen Cohen (Steel), Damian Page (Lancelot), Darren McKay (Frenchy), Elliott Moran (Sevenfold), Zaid Felix (Brute), Briar Truong (Chang), Daniel Hill (Dante), Alex Robles (Terry), Edwin Sparks (Borden), Aron Evans (Scout), Sonny Carson (Bronson), Marco Valentino (Dayton), Glen Beck (Marauder) and Cal Marin (Marcus).

The criminal charges were Kidnapping, Hate Crimes, Racketeer Influenced, and Corrupt Organization Act (RICO). Abusive Sexual Contact, Assault with a Deadly Weapon, Aggravated Assault/Battery, being in possession of a firearm, weapons violations, bombing matters, Conspiracy, Domestic Terrorism, Drug Smuggling, Drug Abuse Violations, Drug Trafficking, Extortion, Forcible Rape, First Degree Murder, Homicide, Hate Crime Acts, Larceny, Molestation, Narcotics violations, Sexual Battery, Racketeering, Possession of Narcotics, Sexual Abuse, Sexual Assault, Stolen Property; Buying, Receiving, or Possessing, Violent Crimes in Aid of Racketeering Activity, and Use of Weapons of Mass Destruction C4.

The Centurions and Crypt Keepers all pled guilty to the following charges. Assault with a Deadly Weapon, Racketeering, Possession of Narcotics, Racketeer influenced and Corrupt Organization Act (RICCO), Violent Crimes in Aid of Racketeering Activity, Stolen Property, Buying, Receiving, or Possessing, Drug Smuggling, Drug Abuse Violations, Drug Trafficking, Extortion, and being in possession of a firearm, and weapon violations.

During the two-year investigation, I'd purchased two hundred pounds of methamphetamine (Crank), four kilos of cocaine, close to one hundred fifty grams of fentanyl, twelve firearms, seven stolen motorcycles, and seventy-five pounds of C4 explosives, and ten grenades. The search warrants recovered an addition forty firearms, seven grenades, 14 kilos of pure cocaine, and an additional hundred pounds of meth. I had closed out eleven murders.

Eight of which were at the hands of Ripper himself. Hatchet and several other Excaliburs who'd murdered the man and his girlfriend at the bar who they also had gang raped.

Several of the Excaliburs received life sentences. Others pled out to ten to twenty years as did The Centurions and the Crypt Keepers. Jimbo was reassigned to DC and promoted as the SAC of Group Two. The AUSA Bryce Cobb was promoted to head of the Organized Crime Bureau in the Eastern District office.

The following members of the Excaliburs were killed or died during the investigation. Arthur Horne (Arthur) serial rapist and murderer, Louis Bowen (Ripper), Brook Joseph (Brooks), Neil Horton (Mohawk), John Higgins (Serpent), and Colten Moss (Whippet).

Cooper Higgins (Lizard) killed the patron at the Cove and was still on the run for that homicide amongst other crimes. The U.S. Marshals were burning the candle at both ends trying to capture him.

During a proffer session, which is a written agreement between the prosecutor and defendant that allows the defendant to give the prosecutor information about an alleged crime while limiting the prosecutor's ability to use that information against the defendant, and possibly give a reduction in his or her sentencing.

Hatchet had asked me, Rogue, oh sorry, "Agent Volpe, whatever happened to the Christmas presents. Did they go off?" I saw the photo's you took of the planted bombs. Did they blow up their clubhouses?"

I said, "Mr. Hatcher, I'm afraid not. What I planted that day in question, was gray modeling clay. It was all a fake to make the Excalibur think I planted the C4. Sorry to disappoint you. It's in your best interest to cooperate with the AUSA or you're never getting out of prison. Do yourself and your family a favor and be a good human being once in your life. Tell him what he needs to know and everything you know about all of Excalibur connections for the guns and narcotics. I'll personally put a good word in for you to the judge."

Hatchet agreed to provide tons of information against many criminal organizations and was placed in protective custody. He received a twenty-year sentence instead of becoming a lifer in prison.

Kelly decided to stay with the Suffolk County PD for one more year. The kids were back home where they belonged and I put my papers in to do a lateral transfer into the DEA. The case ended up being the largest undercover infiltration of an OMG. I knew I had made many enemies in the biker world and there would be a price on my head. Kahuna had taken over the reins of President of The

Guardians chapter in New York. I knew the Guardians would have my family and my back no matter what was thrown at us.

Two months later our lives had gone back to normal. Aside from some new battle scars on my body, all was well. I did on occasion have some floaters in the eye that Ripper's axe had lacerated. We didn't know the extent of the damage until we had gone to the eye doctor. Ripper's axe blade had nicked the top part of my eyeball. The doctor told me I should start wearing an eyepatch to protect it from further damage. I told Kelly that I'd wear it when we wanted to role-play in the bedroom.

Fall of 2024, I took Talia and Ronin for a run and a long walk. As we turned around from our walk, I heard a voice from behind me, say, "Hey Rogue, nice dogs you have there. Mind if we take one? Then the daytime turned black.

An hour later, I felt Talia licking my face and forehead. She was barking and howling loudly. Talia's face and head were covered in someone else's blood. She'd torn someone up badly. I couldn't find Ronin anywhere and I was still dazed and confused from the knock on my head. I remembered seeing the person who spoke to me wearing a Marquis leather vest. The front patch read Lizard.

I texted Kelly and Kahuna with my location and wrote, "911."

THE END